MW00510787

VOCABULARY CONNECTIONS

A Content Area Approach

Program Consultants

Dr. Barbara Coulter
Director, Department of Communication Arts
Detroit Public Schools

Dr. Catherine C. Hatala
Director, Reading/English Language Arts
School District of Philadelphia

STECK-VAUGHN
COMPANY
ELEMENTARY • SECONDARY • ADULT • LIBRARY

Executive Editor: Diane Sharpe
Project Editor: Amanda Johnson Sperry
Assistant Art Director: Richard Balsam
Design Manager: Jim Cauthron
Photo Editor Margie Foster
Product Development: McClanahan & Company, Inc.
Electronic Production: Tracor Publications

ILLUSTRATIONS

Cover: Ed Lindlof
Content Area Logos: Skip Sorvino

Donna Ayers pp. 108–111, 113; Doron Ben-Ami pp. 26, 85–87, 89, 115–116, 118; Nancy Carpenter pp. 38–39, 41; Dr. Leon Chang pp. 78–79; Nancy Didion pp. 32–33, 35; Eldon Doty pp. 54–57, 59, 72–74, 76, 92–92, 94; Leslie Dunlap pp. 18–20, 22, 24–25, 28, 92, 98, 100; Alan Eitzen pp. 60–63; Doris Ettlinger p. 65; Bob Guiliani pp. 103–105, 107; Debbe Heller pp. 7–9, 11; Den Schofield pp. 12–15, 17, 120–122, 124; Freya Tanz pp. 43–44, 46; Jean and Mou-sien Tseng pp. 48–49, 52, 67–68, 70, 80–81.

PHOTOGRAPHY

P. 5 © Tony Freeman/Photo Edit; p. 23 Paul Howell/Gamma-Liaison; p. 26 Mike Powell/Allsport; p. 29 Jeff Gnas/The Stock Market; p. 53 Franco Salmoiragni/The Stock Market; p. 77 Jon Feingersh/The Stock Market; p. 95 Barry King/Gamma-Liaison; p. 96 Archive Photos; p. 97 Fox/Shooting Star; p. 101 Andrew Wood/Photo Researchers.

ACKNOWLEDGMENTS

Harcourt Brace and Company: Excerpts from *The Shark Callers* by Eric Campbell. Copyright © 1994, 1993 by Eric Campbell. First published 1993 by Pan Macmillan Children's Books, London, reprinted by permission of Harcourt Brace and Company.

Harper & Row, Publishers, Inc.: Adapted selection from *Banner In The Sky* by James Ramsey Ullman. (J.B. Lippincott). Copyright © 1954 by James Ramsey Ullman. Reprinted by permission of Harper & Row, Publishers, Inc.

Reeve Lindbergh: "Morning — The Bird Perched for Flight" from *Earth Shine*, copyright © 1966, 1969 by Anne Morrow Lindbergh. Reprinted by permission of Reeve Lindbergh as attorney-in-fact for the author.

Macmillan Publishing Company: Pronunciation Key, reprinted with permission of the publisher from the *Macmillan School Dictionary 2.* Copyright © 1990 Macmillan Publishing Company, a division of Macmillan, Inc.

Charlotte Sheedy Literary Agency, Inc.: "Sun Prairie" from Chapter 1 of *Portrait of an Artist: A Biography of Georgia O'Keeffe* by Laurie Lisle. Copyright © 1980 by Laurie Lisle. Reprinted by the permission of Charlotte Sheedy Literary Agency, Inc.

ISBN 0-8172-6356-X

Copyright © 1997 Steck-Vaughn Company.
All rights reserved. No part of the material protected by this copyright may be reproduced or utilized in any form or by any means, electronic or mechanical, including photocopying, recording, or by any information storage and retrieval system, without permission in writing from the copyright owner. Requests for permission to make copies of any part of the work should be mailed to: Copyright Permissions, Steck-Vaughn Company, P.O. Box 26015, Austin, TX 78755.
Printed in the United States of America.

4 5 6 7 8 9 10 BP 01 00 99 98

TABLE OF CONTENTS

Content Area Symbols

 Literature Social Studies Science Mathematics Health Fine Arts

TABLE OF CONTENTS

STRETCHING BEYOND

All achievers are not alike. Some acquire fame in their pursuit of excellence. Others enjoy quiet victories doing their best to improve their lives.

In Lessons 1–4, you will read about people whose determination led them not only to meet their goals, but to exceed their expectations. Have you read or heard about someone who has achieved a difficult goal? Think about goals that you would like to achieve. What traits help us to reach our goals? Write your ideas on the lines below.

Possible Goals	Traits That Help Us Achieve Goals
_____	_____
_____	_____
_____	_____
_____	_____

★ Read the story below. Think about the meanings of the **boldfaced** words. ★

Dancing Across Time

As a young girl growing up in Chicago in the early 1900s, Katherine Dunham began her **lifelong** study of dance. At first, she studied ballet. Then Dunham became interested in the **contemporary** dances the young black people her own age were creating. An idea struck her. Were these modern dance steps **derived** from dances done by blacks in Africa long ago? She believed these new dances had many movements and rhythms that showed they could be traced to African tribal dances.

To learn more about the history of black dance, Katherine Dunham enrolled at the University of Chicago. There she studied **anthropology**, the science of human cultures or different ways of life. After graduating, she studied black dances of the West Indies islands. She traveled to Jamaica and to Haiti, where many African blacks had been brought as slaves. There she learned folktales, legends, songs, and other **lore** of the blacks.

The native islanders trusted this young student of dance. They allowed her to watch their **ceremonial** dances. These formal, colorful dances were part of an ancient religion that had been brought to the islands by the slaves from Africa. Most of these dances had never been seen by outsiders. As she watched the rhythmic movements, Dunham found the answer to her question. Many modern dance steps had come from ancient ways of dancing.

Katherine Dunham became very **knowledgeable** about the black dances of Haiti and Jamaica. After several years, she decided to bring what she had learned to the stage. At first she performed alone, presenting **authentic** dances as she had seen them done by the islanders. Later she formed her own dance company in the United States. Audiences loved seeing real dances that came from another part of the world. They admired Dunham and her dances for their dramatic, expressive movements.

Katherine Dunham continued her **diligent** study of black culture and dance throughout her life. Her hard, careful work has truly **enriched** the performing arts. Audiences all over the world have been able to experience the beauty, humor, and dignity of black dance by watching her company perform.

★ Go back to the story. Underline the words or sentences that give you a clue to the meaning of each **boldfaced** word. ★

CONTEXT CLUES

Read each pair of sentences. Look for clues to help you complete one of the sentences with a word from the box. Write the word on the line.

contemporary	knowledgeable	lifelong	diligent
derived	anthropology	lore	ceremonial
authentic	enriched		

1. In many groups, the ancient dances are done by everyone. Dancers who are _____ and experienced may help small children learn the steps.

2. Group dancing may continue for hours on end. This is especially true on special _____ occasions.

3. Katherine Dunham carefully watched every step in these long dances. In her _____ way, she made precise notes about each dance.

4. As a student of _____, Dunham was also interested in the folktales and legends of Africa and the West Indies. She kept detailed records about each one that she heard.

5. In her autobiography, Dunham tells how her days in Jamaica _____ her life. By living there for a long time, she gained important insights into ancient customs.

6. From folktales and other _____, Dunham got ideas for dances. Stories and beliefs from the Caribbean could be turned into plays that could be performed by dancers.

7. Dance composers get their ideas from many sources. Dunham _____ her dances from ones she had observed.

8. People in big cities were not used to seeing dances in their original form. They were delighted to see the _____ steps and hear the actual rhythms of old dances in Dunham's performances.

9. Modern audiences are also used to movies and stage shows. Dunham put her dances into these _____ forms.

10. Dunham changed the lives of audiences and dance students. Many of these people developed a _____ interest in black dance.

DICTIONARY SKILLS

Write the words in alphabetical order, one word on each line. Then turn to the Dictionary, beginning on page 133. Find each word in the Dictionary and write its meaning below.

diligent	lifelong	enriched	anthropology
ceremonial	lore	derived	contemporary
knowledgeable	authentic		

1. _____

2. _____

3. _____

4. _____

5. _____

6. _____

7. _____

8. _____

9. _____

10. _____

ANTONYMS

Antonyms are words with opposite meanings. Match the words in the box with their antonyms listed below. Write each word on the line.

contemporary	ceremonial	knowledgeable
lifelong	authentic	diligent

1. ignorant _____

2. fake _____

3. careless _____

4. old-fashioned _____

5. informal _____

6. brief _____

RIDDLE

Why are four-legged animals such poor dancers? To find the answer to this riddle, read each definition below. Write each word from the box next to its definition. Then write each letter on its numbered blank.

lifelong	contemporary	diligent	lore
derived	knowledgeable	authentic	enriched
anthropology	ceremonial		

1. for a special occasion ___ ___ ___ ___ ___ ___ ___ ___ ___ ___
              13   11

2. genuine ___ ___ ___ ___ ___ ___ ___ ___ ___
              2   15

3. the knowledge and stories of a culture ___ ___ ___ ___
         3

4. science that studies people and cultures ___ ___ ___ ___ ___ ___ ___ ___ ___ ___ ___ ___
       18 5

5. added to; made better ___ ___ ___ ___ ___ ___ ___ ___
  17   16

6. modern; up-to-date ___ ___ ___ ___ ___ ___ ___ ___ ___ ___ ___ ___
    1   4

7. lasting a lifetime ___ ___ ___ ___ ___ ___ ___ ___
  12 14

8. thorough; careful ___ ___ ___ ___ ___ ___ ___ ___
        8   9

9. taken from ___ ___ ___ ___ ___ ___ ___
       7

10. well-informed ___ ___ ___ ___ ___ ___ ___ ___ ___ ___ ___ ___ ___
      10   6

ANSWER: ___ ___ ___ ___ ___ ___ ___ ___ ___ ___ ___
      1 2 3 4   5 6 7 8   9 10 11

___ ___ ___ ___ ___ ___ ___ ___ !
12 13 14 15 14 16 17 18

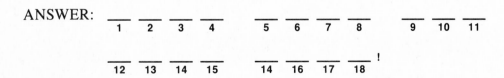

GET WISE TO TESTS

Directions: Read each sentence. Pick the word that best completes the sentence. Mark the answer space for that word.

 Some tests put letters before the answer choices. Be sure to find the letter of the answer you think is correct, then fill in the circle beside it.

1. The _____ student studied long hours for the big exam.
   A ○ equally
   B ○ diligent
   C ○ sometimes
   D ○ lore

2. The old table in the dining room is an _____ antique.
   A ○ enriched
   B ○ origin
   C ○ authentic
   D ○ unusually

3. Davy Crockett is one of the heroes of early Western _____.
   A ○ lore
   B ○ laugh
   C ○ courageous
   D ○ authentic

4. My grandfather has had a _____ interest in stamps.
   A ○ lifelong
   B ○ collect
   C ○ foolishly
   D ○ ceremonial

5. Our class has been _____ by some excellent guest speakers.
   A ○ derived
   B ○ lecture
   C ○ sleepy
   D ○ enriched

6. I prefer _____ music to what my parents listen to.
   A ○ create
   B ○ loudly
   C ○ contemporary
   D ○ anthropology

7. My math teacher is _____ about many subjects in addition to the one he teaches.
   A ○ derived
   B ○ lore
   C ○ produce
   D ○ knowledgeable

8. The ancient high priest put on his _____ robes.
   A ○ ceremonial
   B ○ color
   C ○ knowledgeable
   D ○ confusion

9. Many English words are _____ from Latin.
   A ○ knowledgeable
   B ○ derived
   C ○ between
   D ○ lifelong

10. Martin studied American Indian cultures in his _____ class.
    A ○ afterwards
    B ○ require
    C ○ anthropology
    D ○ authentic

Writing

Think about the differences between old dances and new ones. Recall an old dance you have seen on television or in the movies. Then think about a new dance you have seen or done yourself.

Write a paragraph describing the similarities and differences between them. Provide details to make the differences clear to the reader. Use some vocabulary words in your writing.

_____

_____

_____

_____

_____

_____

Turn to "My Personal Word List" on page 131. Write some words from the story or other words that you would like to know more about. Use a dictionary to find the meanings.

_____

_____

_____

_____

_____

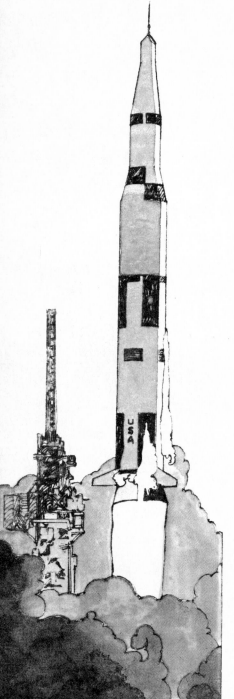

★ Read the story below. Think about the meanings of
the **boldfaced** words. ★

Earth Shine

Anne Morrow Lindbergh, wife of the famous aviator Charles Lindbergh,
had many adventures of her own. Here she describes the magnificent
liftoff of *Apollo 8* from Cape Canaveral, Florida, on
December 21, 1968.

We wake to the alarm at four thirty and leave our motel at five fifteen.
The three astronauts must be already climbing into their seats at the top
of their "thirty-six-story" rocket, poised for flight. The **pilgrimage** of
sightseers has started to the Cape. Already the buses have left and lines
of cars are on the roads. As we approach the Cape we see again the
rocket and its launching tower from far off over the lagoon. It is still
illumined with searchlights, but last night's vision has vanished. It is no
longer tender or biological but simply a machine, the newest and most
perfected creation of a scientific age — hard, weighty material.

We watch the launching with some of the astronauts and their
families, from a site near the Vehicle Assembly Building. Our cars are
parked on a slight rise of ground. People get out, walk about restlessly,
set up cameras, and adjust their binoculars. The launch pad is about
three miles away, near the beach. As dawn flushes the horizon, an egret
rises and lazily glides across the flats between us and the pad. It is a still
morning. Ducks call from nearby inlets. Vapor trails of a high-flying
plane turn pink in an almost cloudless sky. Stars pale in the blue.

With the morning light, Apollo 8 and its launching tower become
clearer, harder, and more defined. One can see the details of
installation. The dark sections on the smooth sides of the rocket,
marking its stages, cut up the single fluid line. Vapor steams furiously
off its side. No longer stark and simple, this morning the rocket is
complicated, mechanical, earth-bound. Too weighty for flight, one
feels.

People stop talking, stand in front of their cars, and raise binoculars
to their eyes. We peer nervously at the launch site and then at our wrist
watches. Radio voices blare unnaturally loud from car windows. "Now
only thirty minutes to launch time . . . fifteen minutes . . . six minutes
. . . thirty seconds to go . . . twenty . . . T minus fifteen . . . fourteen
. . . thirteen . . . twelve . . . eleven . . . ten . . . nine . . . **Ignition!**"

A jet of steam shoots from the pad below the rocket. "Ahhhh!" The
crowd gasps, almost in unison. Now great flames spurt, leap, belch out

across the horizon. Clouds of smoke billow up on either side of the rocket, completely hiding its base. From the midst of this holocaust, the rocket begins to rise – slowly, as in a dream, so slowly it seems to hang suspended on the cloud of fire and smoke. It's impossible – it can't rise. Yes, it rises, but heavily, as if the giant weight is pulled by an invisible hand out of the atmosphere, like the lead on a plumb line from the depths of the sea. Slowly it rises and – because of our distance – silently, as in a dream.

Suddenly the noise breaks, jumps across our three separating miles – a shattering roar of explosions, a trip hammer over one's head, under one's feet, through one's body. The earth shakes; cars rattle; vibrations beat in the chest. A roll of thunder, **prolonged**, prolonged, prolonged. I drop the binoculars and put my hands to my ears, holding my head to keep it steady. My throat tightens – am I going to cry? – my eyes are fixed on the rocket, mesmerized by its slow **ascent**.

The **foreground** is now full of birds; a great flock of ducks, herons, small birds, rise pell-mell from the marshes at the noise. Fluttering in alarm and confusion, they scatter in all directions as if it were the end of the world. In the seconds I take to look at them, the rocket has left the tower.

It is up and away, a comet boring through the sky, no longer the **vulnerable** untried child, no longer the earth-bound machine, or the weight at the end of a line, but sheer terrifying force, blasting upward on its own **titanic** power.

It has gone miles into the sky. It is blurred by a cloud. No, it has made its own cloud – a huge vapor trail, which hides it. Out of the cloud something falls, cartwheeling down, smoking. "The first-stage cutoff," someone says. Where is the rocket itself? There, above the cloud now, reappears the rocket, only a very bright star, **diminishing** every second. Soon out of sight, off to lunar space.

One looks earthward again. It is curiously still and empty. A cloud of brown smoke hangs motionless on the horizon. Its long shadow reaches us across the grass. The launch pad is empty. The abandoned launching tower is being sprayed with jets of water to cool it down. It steams in the bright morning air. Still dazed, people stumble into cars and start the slow, jammed **trek** back to town. The monotone of radio voices continues. One clings to this last thread of contact with something incredibly beautiful that has vanished.

From Earth Shine, by Anne Morrow Lindbergh

★ Go back to the story. Underline any words or sentences that give you clues to the meanings of the **boldfaced** words. ★

13

CONTEXT CLUES

Read each pair of sentences. Look for clues to help you complete one of the sentences with a word from the box. Write the word on the line.

ascent	prolonged	pilgrimage	ignition
trek	installation	foreground	vulnerable
titanic	diminishing		

1. Before dawn, the astronauts arrive at the _____. At this site, for months on end, the shuttle flight has been sitting in preparation.

2. It is always possible that a launch may be delayed. If this happens, the time that the astronauts have to stay in an uncomfortable position will be _____.

3. Even at this point, the astronauts are extremely _____. As they wait, they are sitting above hundreds of tons of explosive rocket fuel.

4. Soon the fuel will be burned to create power. This will happen during _____.

5. A truly _____ power is necessary at lift-off. The gravity is so strong that tremendous force is required to break away from it.

6. This will not be some ordinary, slow _____. It will be a trip of incredible swiftness.

7. Soon the astronauts will travel away from Earth. As they do so, our planet will seem to be _____ in size.

8. The shuttle is programmed to reach a certain altitude and then begin its orbit of Earth. The _____ of the shuttle will end when this point is reached.

9. When the astronauts look away from Earth, they see the moon in the _____. Behind the moon, they see brilliant galaxies.

10. They have never been this far from home before. This is a _____ that will carry them farther than was ever dreamed possible.

WORD ORIGINS

Knowing the origin of a word can help you understand its meaning. Read each word origin. Then write each word from the box next to its origin.

ascent	**titanic**	**diminishing**	**vulnerable**
trek	**prolonged**	**ignition**	

1. from Latin <u>ascendere</u>, to climb _____

2. from Latin <u>ignire</u>, to set on fire _____

3. from Latin <u>dēminuere</u>, to lessen _____

4. from Greek <u>Titans</u>, huge and powerful gods _____

5. from Dutch <u>trecken</u>, to pull or travel _____

6. from Latin <u>vulnerare</u>, to wound _____

7. from Latin <u>pro</u>, forward + <u>longus</u>, long _____

CLOZE PARAGRAPH

Use the words in the box to complete the paragraph. Then reread the paragraph to be sure it makes sense.

foreground	**diminishing**	**installation**
pilgrimage	**ignition**	

The Space Camp in Huntsville, Alabama, allows students to experience how astronauts are trained. Students take part in activities similar to the experiences an astronaut has. In one activity, they feel a

rocket's power begin during (1) _____. Classes

include seeing an (2) _____ site where the rocket is prepared. One exhibit allows students to pretend they are making a

(3) _____ into outer space that is almost like the real

thing. They watch Earth (4) _____ as their rocket travels farther and farther into space. The home planet is no longer in

the (5) _____. The moon lies straight ahead.

GET WISE TO TESTS

Directions: Fill in the space for the word that fits best in the sentence.

Be sure to mark the answer space correctly. Do <u>not</u> mark the circle with an X or with a checkmark (✔). Instead, fill in the circle neatly and completely with your pencil.

1. The plane climbed toward the clouds. We watched its _____.
   (A) project   (C) ascent
   (B) installation   (D) attempt

2. They moved farther away with the flashlight. John saw its light _____.
   (A) diminishing   (C) smiling
   (B) stalking   (D) escaping

3. The play began late. We grew impatient during the _____ wait.
   (A) shortened   (C) prolonged
   (B) intended   (D) entered

4. At noon, the hikers rested at the peak. They had begun their _____ at dawn.
   (A) lore   (C) ignition
   (B) search   (D) trek

5. The white house was behind the bright maple. The color in the _____ seemed to shine.
   (A) foreground   (C) frame
   (B) kitchen   (D) ascent

6. We go to the rocket _____ early to see the lift-off.
   (A) employee   (C) instruction
   (B) installation   (D) foreground

7. The memorial is famous. Many people make a _____ to visit it.
   (A) memory   (C) marble
   (B) discovery   (D) pilgrimage

8. The man can lift a refrigerator. He has _____ strength.
   (A) vulnerable   (C) titanic
   (B) intelligent   (D) sturdy

9. Roses will die in the cold. They are _____ and must be covered.
   (A) vulnerable   (C) small
   (B) prolonged   (D) lifelong

10. The can of gas exploded. The _____ was caused by a careless smoker.
   (A) pilgrimage   (C) mystery
   (B) ignition   (D) reason

Review

1. This _____ furniture was designed for the modern teenager.
   (A) contemporary   (C) independent
   (B) old-fashioned   (D) ambitious

2. Chris is an art expert and is _____ about music, too.
   (A) knowledgeable   (C) expectant
   (B) sizeable   (D) amusing

3. Outsiders are not allowed to watch some American Indian _____ dances.
   (A) diligent   (C) ceremonial
   (B) collective   (D) fast

4. Marge will _____ a new recipe for soup from her grandmother's old recipes.
   (A) persist   (C) skip
   (B) derive   (D) boil

Writing

The logbook entries of travelers tell about events in the sequence in which they actually happen. Imagine that you and a classmate are the astronauts in the space capsule shown here.

Write a logbook entry that describes an exciting moment during your flight. In sequential order, tell what you experience and how you feel. Use some vocabulary words in your writing.

Date: _____

Entry: _____

_____

_____

_____

_____

_____

_____

_____

_____

_____

_____

_____

_____

_____

_____

_____

_____

_____

_____

Turn to "My Personal Word List" on page 131. Write some words from the story or other words that you would like to know more about. Use a dictionary to find the meanings.

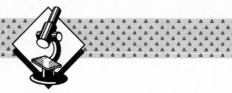

★ Read the story below. Think about the meanings of the **boldfaced** words. ★

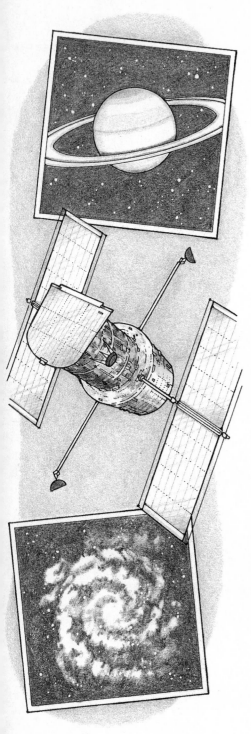

New Views of the Universe

Some three hundred eighty miles above the earth, the Hubble Space Telescope orbits our planet once every ninety-five minutes. With Hubble, scientists can **probe** the universe. They explore it by studying the pictures Hubble sends to Earth. The pictures give scientists detailed and revealing pictures of events in the **cosmos**. Scientists have used satellites as part of their investigation of space ever since the 1970s. Hubble, which is a special kind of satellite, is helping scientists in this great **inquiry**.

The Hubble telescope was launched by the United States from a space shuttle in 1990. Before that, scientists had tried to **analyze** space by using telescopes on Earth. Their careful study proved to be very difficult. The images they saw were blurred because Earth's atmosphere bends light from the stars and galaxies. Hubble promised a clearer look at outer space. Hubble's main mirror was flawed, however, and the pictures it sent back were out of focus.

In 1993, the National Aeronautics and Space Administration (NASA) sent a crew of astronauts to fix Hubble. The astronauts did a perfect job. Since then, Hubble has helped scientists make some major discoveries. Hubble has photographed two new moons on the planet Saturn. It has shown that stars other than the sun have planets. It is helping scientists find the answers to some important questions. For example, it is helping them **ascertain** how the universe began and how old it is.

People argue about space exploration, a **controversial** subject. Some people think we should not investigate space while there are serious problems on our own planet. They believe the program costs too much.

Other people think the exploration of space is **inevitable**. They feel it is bound to happen. They argue that people are natural explorers who are excited by the vastness, the **immensity**, of space. People in favor of space exploration believe that what we learn from space is priceless and that **invaluable** information can be gathered by space satellites. They also feel there is no limit to what we can learn in space. For them, the universe is a source of **infinite** knowledge, and the Hubble Space Telescope is a key to the secrets of the universe.

★ Go back to the story. Underline the words or sentences that give you a clue to the meaning of each **boldfaced** word. ★

USING CONTEXT

Meanings for the vocabulary words are given below. Go back to the story and read each sentence that has a vocabulary word. If you still cannot tell the meaning, look for clues in the sentences that come before and after the one with the vocabulary word. Write each word in front of its meaning.

ascertain	inevitable	cosmos	invaluable
immensity	analyze	probe	controversial
inquiry	infinite		

1. _____ : to study carefully

2. _____ : great size

3. _____ : the universe; all of space

4. _____ : to explore

5. _____ : certain to happen

6. _____ : endless

7. _____ : causing questions and arguments

8. _____ : research; investigation

9. _____ : priceless

10. _____ : to find out

CHALLENGE YOURSELF

Name two things that are inevitable in your daily life.

_____   _____

Name two animals known for their immensity.

_____   _____

Name two things you consider to be invaluable.

_____   _____

Name two things about the future that you would like to ascertain.

_____   _____

DICTIONARY SKILLS

The **pronunciation key** in a dictionary explains how a word is said aloud. Study the pronunciation key below. Then look at the five vocabulary words and their pronunciations. Answer each question by writing the correct word or words.

a	at	i	it	u	up
ā	ape	ī	ice	o͞o	food
e	end	o	hot	ch	chin
ē	me	ō	old		

ə { a in about
e in taken
i in pencil
o in lemon
u in circus

im•men•si•ty (i men´si tē)   **cos•mos** (koz´məs, koz´mōs)
probe (prōb)   **in•ev•i•ta•ble** (in ev´i tə bəl)
in•fi•nite (in´fə nit)

1. Which word has the same e sound as me? _____

2. Which word has the same o sound as hot? _____

3. Which word has the k sound of c? _____

4. Which three words have the same i sound as in it? _____

_____   _____

REWRITING SENTENCES

Rewrite each sentence using one of the vocabulary words from the box.

controversial	analyze	invaluable	ascertain

1. My brother's help on this project was extremely valuable.

_____

2. Once we have all of the information, we will study it very carefully.

_____

3. The team's decision to elect a captain was argued about endlessly.

_____

4. We need to find out how many people are coming to dinner.

_____

Directions: Choose the word that best takes the place of the boldfaced word.

This test will show how well you understand the meaning of the words. Think about the meaning of the boldfaced word before you choose your answer.

1. The scientist wanted to **analyze** the plants. He wanted to know why one died in the frost and the other didn't.
   - (A) defeat
   - (B) exhaust
   - (C) shrink
   - (D) study

2. The nation's budget is a **controversial** issue. Some people want it cut, and others want spending increased.
   - (A) invaluable
   - (B) mysterious
   - (C) disputed
   - (D) forbidden

3. How large is the **cosmos**? This may be a question we cannot answer with a telescope.
   - (A) foreground
   - (B) planet
   - (C) universe
   - (D) sun

4. The questions went on and on. There seemed to be an **infinite** number of them.
   - (A) accurate
   - (B) endless
   - (C) important
   - (D) inevitable

5. My parents' advice is often **invaluable**. It's saved me from making some big mistakes.
   - (A) priceless
   - (B) confusing
   - (C) diminishing
   - (D) fascinating

6. The **immensity** of the dinosaurs is astonishing. Some could tower over modern buildings.
   - (A) appetite
   - (B) ascent
   - (C) cosmos
   - (D) hugeness

7. The **inquiry** into the man's disappearance was useless. We still don't know where he is.
   - (A) test
   - (B) riddle
   - (C) search
   - (D) solution

8. The student could not **ascertain** the answer. None of the books he referred to gave it.
   - (A) find out
   - (B) make up
   - (C) write in
   - (D) ignore

9. A surgeon knows how to **probe** the human body. Yet he does this without injuring the patient.
   - (A) destroy
   - (B) improve
   - (C) ascertain
   - (D) explore

10. It was almost **inevitable** that the home team would win. They had won every game that season.
   - (A) impossible
   - (B) certain
   - (C) infinite
   - (D) amusing

Writing

What is your opinion on space exploration? Do you think that the discoveries made by the Hubble telescope and other space explorations are worth the cost? Or are there better ways for the government to use that money?

Write a paragraph that either supports the space program or explains how the money could be better used on Earth. Use some vocabulary words in your writing.

Turn to "My Personal Word List" on page 131. Write some words from the story or other words that you would like to know more about. Use a dictionary to find the meanings.

★ Read the story below. Think about the meanings of
the **boldfaced** words. ★

Setting Her Own Course

In the **marathon**, runners travel more than twenty-six miles over open country. A top-flight runner can complete this long-distance race in about two and one-half hours, but it is **agonizing** for even an experienced runner. Runners become exhausted, they develop muscle cramps and soreness, and they may collapse from dizziness or fatigue. **Adverse** weather conditions – wind, rain, and extreme cold or heat – can add to the challenge. Often, only people with a special **aptitude**, or natural ability, choose to run marathons. The difficulties **dishearten** many athletes. However, marathon runners are not easily discouraged.

Cathy O'Brien of New Hampshire has been competing in long-distance races since she was thirteen. From the beginning, she showed her strength and energy by running the whole course. She had the **stamina** to run long races. She also had the desire to **excel**, to set new time records.

O'Brien competed in the first women's Olympic Marathon Trials when she was only sixteen. By far the youngest runner, she surprised everyone by finishing ninth in a field of more than two hundred. Four years later, she placed third in the U.S. Trials and went on to the Olympics in Seoul, Korea, where she finished fortieth. In her third try at the Olympics, she finished second in the U.S. Trials and tenth in the world. She paid a heavy price for her achievement, though. She competed with a hamstring injury. After the race, the pain in her leg was **acute**. It hurt so much that she couldn't run a step for four months. She made sure that she had fully recovered before she began training for the 1996 Olympics in Atlanta, Georgia.

Ordinarily O'Brien is an easy-going person, but in a race she is different. She is an **aggressive** runner. She loves to compete, and she runs to win. She decides which races she will enter and how she will train. Praise is not important to her. Winning the **acclaim** of everyone is not why she runs.

Describing her feelings about running, O'Brien says, "I come off as a mellow person. Some might think I don't care. But once the starting gun goes off, I become a different person. I don't run marathons because it's a job or because that's what others have done. I've been doing it so long that the marathon's like another part of me."

★ Go back to the story. Underline the words or sentences that give you a clue to the meaning of each **boldfaced** word. ★

USING CONTEXT

Meanings for the vocabulary words are given below. Go back to the story and read each sentence that contains a vocabulary word. If you still cannot tell the meaning, look for clues in the sentences that come before and after the one with the vocabulary word. Write each word in front of its meaning.

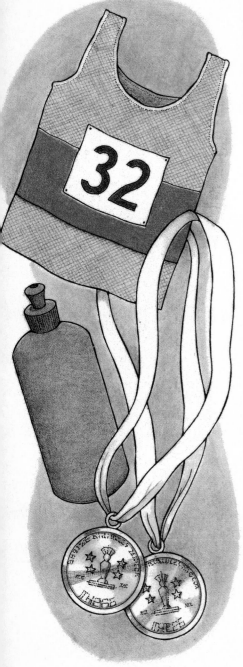

aptitude	acclaim	adverse	acute
agonizing	marathon	dishearten	excel
aggressive	stamina		

1. _____: an extremely long race or contest

2. _____: a natural talent, ability, or capacity

3. _____: be better or do better than others

4. _____: physical strength or endurance

5. _____: enthusiastic approval; high praise

6. _____: not favorable; harmful

7. _____: sharp and severe; critical

8. _____: cause to lose hope; discourage

9. _____: causing great suffering

10. _____: energetic and forceful

CHALLENGE YOURSELF

Name two sports in which you need stamina.

_____   _____

Name two problems that you consider to be acute in today's world.

_____   _____

Name two situations that can dishearten a student.

_____   _____

Name two activities that you would like to excel in.

_____   _____

WORD GROUPS

Read each pair of words. Think about how they are alike. Write the word from the box that best completes each group.

marathon	dishearten	excel	adverse	aggressive
acclaim	aptitude	acute	stamina	

1. unfavorable, harmful, _____

2. ability, knack, _____

3. exceed, outdo, _____

4. energetic, forceful, _____

5. strength, endurance, _____

6. severe, extreme, _____

7. discourage, unnerve, _____

8. applause, praise, _____

9. relay, sprint, _____

ANTONYMS

Remember that **antonyms** are words with opposite meanings. Match the words in the box with their antonyms below. Write each word on the line.

agonizing	acclaim	dishearten	excel
aggressive	stamina	adverse	acute

1. dull _____

2. encourage _____

3. painless _____

4. timid _____

5. fail _____

6. disapproval _____

7. tiredness _____

8. favorable _____

WORD ORIGINS

Knowing the origin of a word can help you understand its meaning. Read each word origin. Then write each word from the box next to its origin.

acclaim	adverse	aggressive	excel	aptitude
acute	agonizing			

1. from the Latin *excellere*, to raise up _____

2. from the Latin *acutus*, sharp _____

3. from the Greek *agonia*, struggle _____

4. from the Latin *aptitudo*, fitness _____

5. from the Latin *advertere*, turn toward angrily _____

6. from the Latin *aggressio*, a going toward _____

7. from the Latin *acclamare*, to shout applause _____

CONNOTATIONS

Some words are very close in meaning, yet there is a small difference between them. The words suggest slightly different things. That is, the words have different **connotations**. Read each sentence below. Choose a word from the box that has a slightly different connotation from the underlined word. Write the vocabulary word on the line.

dishearten	stamina	acclaim	aggressive	marathon

1. He has the ability to run well, but he may lack the _____ to make it through the whole race.

2. She is vigorous and certain of her goal, but she is not _____ enough to pursue it.

3. It was a tough contest, but not long enough or hard enough to be called a _____.

4. Losing the race upset her, but she will not let this setback _____ her.

5. They had hoped to win national _____, but they had to be satisfied with a round of applause from the audience.

Directions: Mark the space for the letter of the word that best completes the sentence.

Before you choose your answer, try reading the sentence with each answer choice. This will help you choose an answer that makes sense.

1. If you **excel** in something, you do _____ in it.
   - (A) poorly
   - (B) well
   - (C) average
   - (D) nothing

2. If you have an **aptitude** for a sport, you should _____ it.
   - (A) avoid
   - (B) support
   - (C) watch
   - (D) play

3. A _____ is an **adverse** weather condition.
   - (A) light breeze
   - (B) misty rain
   - (C) blizzard
   - (D) warm temperature

4. An **acute** pain would be very _____.
   - (A) dull
   - (B) mild
   - (C) sharp
   - (D) short

5. A rainy day might **dishearten** someone going to a _____.
   - (A) movie
   - (B) store
   - (C) library
   - (D) picnic

6. A **marathon** runner runs for _____ distances.
   - (A) long
   - (B) several
   - (C) short
   - (D) complete

7. **Acclaim** for a job well done is usually in the form of _____.
   - (A) letters
   - (B) strength
   - (C) hissing
   - (D) praise

8. An **agonizing** disease is one that is quite _____.
   - (A) painful
   - (B) unusual
   - (C) ugly
   - (D) common

9. To increase your **stamina**, you must _____ a lot.
   - (A) exercise
   - (B) smile
   - (C) probe
   - (D) interpret

10. **Aggressive** people often do _____ they have to.
    - (A) less than
    - (B) the same as
    - (C) more than
    - (D) nothing

Review

1. On **ignition**, something _____.
   - (A) tramples
   - (B) reflects
   - (C) burns
   - (D) fades

2. To **enrich** something, you must _____.
   - (A) bow
   - (B) add
   - (C) ascertain
   - (D) sing

3. To be **infinite**, something would have to be _____.
   - (A) outstanding
   - (B) inevitable
   - (C) dirty
   - (D) endless

4. A subject that is **controversial** is one that people _____ about.
   - (A) play
   - (B) see
   - (C) argue
   - (D) wonder

Writing

Do you have a favorite sport that you feel strongly about, as Cathy O'Brien does about running the marathon? Or do you have a favorite hobby or free-time activity?

Write about your favorite sport or other activity. Tell what it involves, why you like it, how you try to improve, and what your goals are. Use some vocabulary words in your writing.

_____

_____

_____

_____

_____

_____

_____

_____

_____

_____

_____

_____

_____

_____

_____

_____

_____

_____

_____

_____

_____

_____

_____

Turn to "My Personal Word List" on page 131. Write some words from the story or other words that you would like to know more about. Use a dictionary to find the meanings.

★ To review the words in Lessons 1–4, turn to page 125. ★

ART TALKS

Throughout time, people have expressed their views of life in artwork. Many great artists have revealed their distinct experiences through their work.

In Lessons 5–8, you will read about some famous artists and works of art. What art activities do you enjoy? What would you create if you felt joyful? How would you show sadness? Write your ideas on the lines below.

Enjoyable Art Activities   **Feelings Shared Through Art**

_____   _____

_____   _____

_____   _____

_____   _____

_____   _____

★ Read the story below. Think about the meanings of the **boldfaced** words. ★

Portrait in Black

It has been said that one picture is worth a thousand words. But when an artist paints a picture, he or she can do more than just copy people and places as they appear in real life. The artist can express personal feelings by the choice of colors and shapes and by the way people and objects are positioned in the picture. In this way, the artist can **emphasize** his or her view of life.

Jacob Lawrence uses his art to **convey** his feelings about being black in America. For example, he portrays the lively energy of a modern black family through bright colors and sharp-edged shapes. When you look at his picture, "The Family," you can feel the power of the family and of the builders in the background who are creating the world of tomorrow. But other paintings, like "Canada Bound," express sad emotions. You can feel the despair and **melancholy** of slavery in the huddled forms of blacks trying to flee to Canada and to freedom more than a century ago.

Jacob Lawrence grew up in Harlem in New York City in the 1920s and 1930s. He saw poverty and misery, but he also experienced the hope and striving of black people. Lawrence was lucky enough to get formal training in art from professional artists who taught in Harlem. His **informal** training came from the life he saw around him and from the freedom he was given to try out his own ideas.

Lawrence decided to become an artist because he wanted to "talk" to people through his art. He wanted to teach and **enlighten** others about black people and their way of life. He wanted to awaken the **conscience** of all Americans and make them feel and think about the struggles of black people for equality and justice.

Lawrence had the rich **legacy**, or heritage, of black history in America to draw on. He created a series of **biographical** paintings of Harriet Tubman and Frederick Douglass, two former slaves who spoke out against slavery. The paintings portray important events in their lives and reflect their **ardent**, passionate feelings that slavery must come to an end. His **graphic** paintings of black Americans remind us in a very real way of the obstacles they have overcome.

★ Go back to the story. Underline the words or sentences that give you a clue to the meaning of each **boldfaced** word. ★

CONTEXT CLUES

Read each pair of sentences. Look for clues to help you complete one of
the sentences with a word from the box. Write the word on the line.

melancholy	enlighten	legacy	ardent
emphasize	graphic	convey	biographical
conscience	informal		

1. Jacob Lawrence became an artist during the Depression in the
   1930s. This _____ detail helps to explain why
   social problems are a theme in his art.

2. Lawrence learned important technical skills from other artists.
   The ideas for his paintings, however, were original and came from
   an _____ study of life around him.

3. His "Migration" paintings show the harsh details of Southern
   blacks migrating north. These paintings are so
   _____ that they gained Lawrence much attention.

4. Part of the series was printed in *Fortune* magazine. Lawrence was
   able to _____ his message to millions.

5. During the 1960s, Lawrence became an _____
   fighter in the battle for civil rights. He was eager to see these rights
   gained for all.

6. Lawrence used his artistic skills to publicize the fight for justice.
   He wanted to _____ the need for social change.

7. Through his paintings, he showed the evil of denying blacks their
   rights. His moral stand helped to stir the _____
   of the nation.

8. Lawrence teaches at the University of Washington. In his class
   lectures he tries to _____ his students about the
   power of art.

9. The injustice that still exists does not discourage him. He refuses
   to give in to _____.

10. Lawrence's paintings have become a living part of the great
    _____ of black history. His paintings show the
    strength of black culture.

DICTIONARY SKILLS

An **entry** in a dictionary has several parts. Read the dictionary entries below. Use these entries to answer the questions.

entry word in syllables	pronunciation	part of speech	definition	derived form

ar·dent (är′dənt) *adj.* Passionate. *adv.* **ar·dent·ly**
graph·ic (graf′ik) *adj.* Vivid; detailed.
con·vey (kən vā′) *v.* To show; express.
in·for·mal (in fôr′məl) *adj.* Not professional. *adv.* **in·for·mal·ly**
leg·a·cy (leg′ə sē) *n.* **leg·a·cies** Heritage.

1. Which words have two different meanings? _____

   _____

2. Which entry includes the plural form? _____

3. Which adjectives can be made into adverbs? _____

   _____

WORD DESCRIPTIONS

Read each word description. Then write the word from the box that best fits each description. Refer to the Dictionary, beginning on page 133, if you need help.

emphasize	ardent	melancholy	conscience	biographical

1. _____ You might use this word to describe strong feelings.

2. _____ This is what you do when you say one word louder than others in the sentence.

3. _____ A book that tells about a real person's life is classified under this heading.

4. _____ If a rainy day makes you sad, you might use this word to describe your feeling.

5. _____ This is what might prevent you from doing something wrong or illegal.

CROSSWORD PUZZLE

Use the definitions and the words in the box to complete the crossword puzzle.

melancholy	enlighten	biographical	ardent
emphasize	legacy	conscience	graphic
convey	informal		

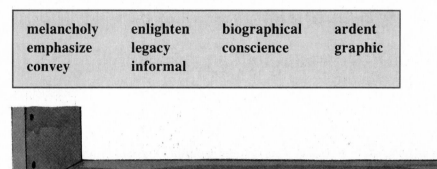

Across
2. eager; enthusiastic
4. stress; make important
5. sadness or gloom
7. having to do with a person's life story
9. sense of right and wrong
10. striking; vivid

Down
1. something handed down from ancestors
3. inform
6. express
8. casual

GET WISE TO TESTS

Directions: Read the sentences. Look for the best word to use in the blank. Mark the answer space for your choice.

Read carefully. Use the other words in the sentences to help you choose the missing word.

1. The speaker pounded the table as he spoke. The audience listened to his _____ speech.
   - (A) dignified
   - (B) ardent
   - (C) long
   - (D) boring

2. The teacher wrote the name on the chalkboard. She wanted to _____ her point.
   - (A) associate
   - (B) lecture
   - (C) grow
   - (D) emphasize

3. The bank clerk gave Jackie too much money by mistake. Later, she returned it because her _____ troubled her.
   - (A) trek
   - (B) conscience
   - (C) legs
   - (D) dog

4. The students knew nothing about the upcoming election. The teacher said he would try to _____ them on the subject.
   - (A) manage
   - (B) enlighten
   - (C) recommend
   - (D) visit

5. Ralph told a ghost story by the campfire. Shivers ran down my spine because it was so _____.
   - (A) clumsy
   - (B) precise
   - (C) graphic
   - (D) amusing

6. The patient wouldn't leave his room and refused to see any visitors. He was very _____.
   - (A) melancholy
   - (B) hungry
   - (C) interesting
   - (D) happy

7. In this poem, the poet writes about the beautiful leaves. He tries to _____ his feelings about autumn.
   - (A) accept
   - (B) prove
   - (C) photograph
   - (D) convey

8. The U.S. Constitution was written by our country's founders. It is a lasting _____ for all Americans.
   - (A) installation
   - (B) legacy
   - (C) nation
   - (D) parent

9. Diane wrote about Vincent van Gogh's life. Her teacher praised her _____ essay.
   - (A) biographical
   - (B) personal
   - (C) expensive
   - (D) unexpected

10. Everyone wore jeans and T-shirts to Juan's party. It was an _____ event.
    - (A) explosive
    - (B) original
    - (C) informal
    - (D) magnetic

Writing

Jacob Lawrence did biographical paintings of Harriet Tubman and Frederick Douglass. A biographical painting shows events in the subject's life, what she or he believed, and the artist's feelings about the person.

Describe a biographical painting about yourself. Use the boxes below to organize your ideas. List what is important to you. Include people, things, and ideas. Also list the feelings you want to convey about yourself to someone looking at this painting. Use your notes to describe how you will depict the events, ideas, and feelings in your painting. Use some vocabulary words in your writing.

Important Events in My Life	What Is Important to Me	Feelings I Want to Convey
_____	_____	_____
_____	_____	_____
_____	_____	_____
_____	_____	_____
_____	_____	_____

_____

_____

_____

_____

_____

_____

_____

_____

_____

_____

_____

_____

Turn to "My Personal Word List" on page 131. Write some words from the story or other words that you would like to know more about. Use a dictionary to find the meanings.

★ Read the story below. Think about the meanings of the **boldfaced** words. ★

Portrait of an Artist

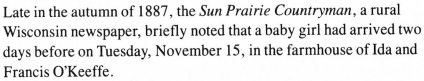

Georgia O'Keeffe's extraordinary paintings of nature made her the first world-famous American woman artist. But what inspired her to dare, at a time when no woman artist was taken seriously?

Late in the autumn of 1887, the *Sun Prairie Countryman*, a rural Wisconsin newspaper, briefly noted that a baby girl had arrived two days before on Tuesday, November 15, in the farmhouse of Ida and Francis O'Keeffe.

Georgia was born into a rapidly **industrializing** world. The country's longest suspension bridge, linking Brooklyn to Manhattan, had recently opened, and the Eiffel Tower in Paris was still under construction, due to be completed in two years.

Little of this **turmoil** affected the **pastoral** life on the Sun Prairie farm, however. It remained like farm life everywhere, suspended in a **timeless ritual** governed by the rhythms of nature. The newborn baby was kept indoors during the long, dark, icy northern winter. When the snow finally melted, the sunlight became warm, and the prairie was touched by the bright green of spring, Georgia was carried outside for the first time. She was placed on a handmade patchwork quilt spread on the new grass and propped up by pillows. Those very first moments of seeing in the brilliant sunlight became indelibly etched in her memory: She precisely remembered the quilt's patterns of flowers on black and tiny red stars as well as the startling blond looks of her mother's friend.

As Georgia became old enough to wander beyond the wide lawn around the white colonial-style O'Keeffe farmhouse, she began to discover the wonders of her father's farm.

The rotation of the seasons, each with its dramatic changes, forced open all of the perceptive child's senses, and they absorbed the marvel of it all. She learned that metal stuck to her fingers in the bitter cold and that flower petals felt velvety soft. She tasted the sweet spring grasses, listened to the high notes of the songbirds, and carefully observed the **profusion** of brilliantly colored wildflowers that appeared when the meadows thawed each year. She remembered the squares of dark, rich, moist earth where a plow had turned the soil, the patterns that were created when neat rows of green seedlings began to sprout, and the wide wheat fields that gilded the land in midsummer. In the fall, the

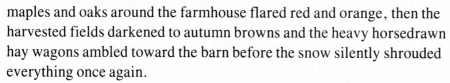

maples and oaks around the farmhouse flared red and orange, then the harvested fields darkened to autumn browns and the heavy horsedrawn hay wagons ambled toward the barn before the snow silently shrouded everything once again.

The country days of her childhood, beginning with daybreak and ending when darkness fell, left Georgia with a **profound** feeling for the companionship of nature and an acute **sensitivity** to its moods.

One day when she was twelve, Georgia asked her friend Lena, the daughter of the O'Keeffes' washerwoman, what she wanted to be when she grew up. Lena replied that she didn't know. "Well, I'm going to be an artist," Georgia blurted out. She was surprised at the sureness of her own words, and she stood silently for a few moments, contemplating their barely perceived meaning.

In **retrospect**, Georgia never precisely put her finger on what prompted her at such an untried age to declare her intent to be an artist. No great women artists were mentioned in her school books, she didn't know any professional artists, and she cared little for the few paintings she had seen.

"I decided that the only thing I could do that was nobody else's business was to paint," she liked to say in adulthood. "I could do as I chose because no one would care."

Even though the United States Senate had rejected an attempt to grant women the right to vote the year Georgia was born, she did not grow up feeling limited by her sex. From a young age she understood that it was both possible and a fine thing to become a professional woman as well as a mother.

At any rate, throughout her life she was unashamed of her womanhood and refused to accept the traditional role assigned to her gender.

In later years, Georgia realized that the most dominant and wholesome aspect of her makeup emerged from her middle western background. "The barn is a very healthy part of me," she wrote several decades later to a collector about her painting of a red Wisconsin barn. Believing that the prairies were the "normal" part of the country, she found it impossible to talk about America to those who did not know them. When she moved to New York and her rural roots appeared remarkable to the **urbanites**, she never lost her belief in their normalcy and her feeling of blessedness at having been born a farmer's daughter in the American Midwest.

From Portrait of an Artist: A Biography of Georgia O'Keeffe, by Laurie Lisle

★ Go back to the story. Underline any words or sentences that give you clues to the meanings of the **boldfaced** words. ★

USING CONTEXT

Meanings for the vocabulary words are given below. Go back to the story and read each sentence that contains a vocabulary word. If you still cannot tell the meaning, look for clues in the sentences that come before and after the one with the vocabulary word. Write each word in front of its meaning.

turmoil	urbanites	retrospect	profusion
ritual	sensitivity	profound	industrializing
pastoral	timeless		

1. _____: creating a large number of factories in a region or a country

2. _____: people who live in a city

3. _____: not affected by the passage of time; eternal

4. _____: state of confused commotion; chaos

5. _____: having the simpleness and beauty of the country

6. _____: intense

7. _____: large amount; abundance

8. _____: thoughtful considering of past events

9. _____: event carried out over and over, usually in the same manner each time

10. _____: quality of having the ability to receive impressions from outside ourselves

CHALLENGE YOURSELF

Name two things that might be pictured in a pastoral scene.

_____   _____

Name two things that can happen when a country is in turmoil.

_____   _____

Name two things you might see a profusion of in a jungle.

_____   _____

WORD ORIGINS

Knowing the origin of a word can help you understand its meaning.
Read each word origin. Then write each word from the box next to
its origin.

industrializing	ritual	retrospect	urbanites

1. from the Latin <u>retro</u>, backward _____

2. from the Latin <u>ritus</u>, custom _____

3. from the Latin <u>urbanus</u>, city _____

4. from the Latin <u>industria</u>, hard work
   or diligence _____

REWRITING SENTENCES

Rewrite each sentence using one of the vocabulary words from the box.

turmoil	pastoral	timeless	profusion
profound	sensitivity	urbanites	

1. The changing of the seasons is an event that is unaffected by the
   passage of time.

   _____

2. He had a deeply felt respect for his parents.

   _____

3. Her condition of being keenly aware of sounds caused her to avoid
   loud restaurants.

   _____

4. The speaker was surprised at the abundance of questions.

   _____

5. The civil war threw their country into a state of commotion.

   _____

6. She enjoyed showing the people from the city her country home.

   _____

7. I long to live in a place that has the simpleness of the country.

   _____

39

GET WISE TO TESTS

Directions: Read each sentence. Pick the word that best completes the sentence. Mark the answer space for that word.

If you are not sure which word completes the sentence, do the best you can. Try to choose the answer that makes the most sense.

1. The _____ in the arena caused the game to be canceled.
   A ○ playing   C ○ retrospect
   B ○ turmoil   D ○ awkward

2. He likes both _____ and country dwellers.
   A ○ profusion   C ○ urbanites
   B ○ insects   D ○ silent

3. Her _____ to sound makes her a better musician.
   A ○ sensitivity   C ○ love
   B ○ pastoral   D ○ strumming

4. In a country that is _____, there are many new jobs.
   A ○ poor   C ○ urbanites
   B ○ richly   D ○ industrializing

5. In _____, he approved of what the mayor had done in the past.
   A ○ ritual   C ○ future
   B ○ destroying   D ○ retrospect

6. The _____ scene in the painting showed cows and horses.
   A ○ pastoral   C ○ lazily
   B ○ turmoil   D ○ careless

7. It was a _____ story that could have happened any time.
   A ○ sleepy   C ○ sensitivity
   B ○ timeless   D ○ book

8. The ceremony was a _____ that was performed yearly.
   A ○ memory   C ○ pastoral
   B ○ visiting   D ○ ritual

9. The _____ of bright colors was lovely to behold.
   A ○ profound   C ○ seeing
   B ○ profusion   D ○ circling

10. She had a _____ love of children that was moving to see.
   A ○ profound   C ○ ritual
   B ○ little   D ○ tenderly

Review

1. She gave a _____ description of the fight.
   A ○ growing   C ○ replacement
   B ○ graphic   D ○ legacy

2. His _____ speech was so moving that it won everyone's support.
   A ○ entertain   C ○ lousy
   B ○ following   D ○ ardent

3. They handed down a _____ of honest government to the next generation.
   A ○ repetition   C ○ historical
   B ○ legacy   D ○ trailing

4. After she stole the candy, her _____ bothered her.
   A ○ condition   C ○ head
   B ○ ardent   D ○ conscience

Writing

Georgia O'Keeffe is most famous for painting huge flowers that filled the canvas. She probably painted these because of her childhood in the country. But during her life she also lived in cities, and she painted city scenes. Look at the two paintings on this page. Think about how they are alike and how they are different. Think about what you know about the city and the country to help make your comparisons.

On the lines below, write two paragraphs. In the first, point out ways the two paintings are alike. In the second paragraph, discuss how they are different. Use some vocabulary words in your writing.

_____

_____

_____

_____

_____

_____

_____

_____

_____

_____

Turn to "My Personal Word List" on page 131. Write some words from the story or other words that you would like to know more about. Use a dictionary to find the meanings.

41

★ Read the story below. Think about the meanings of the **boldfaced** words. ★

Buried Treasure

Have you ever dreamed of going on a trip to a place where ancient treasures are buried? Many people dream of becoming **archaeologists**, scientists who study the ancient past. They picture themselves going on a dig in Greece. There they would **excavate** the ruins of a temple from under the earth where it was buried two thousand years ago. Others dream of going to Egypt and finding a true **bonanza** — an untouched pyramid. They would become famous for bringing its golden treasures to light for all the world to see.

This dream came true for a team of archaeologists who discovered a temple in Mexico City in 1978. It was the Great Temple of the Aztecs. The Aztecs were an Indian civilization that lived from the 1200s to the time the Spanish conquered Mexico in the sixteenth century. Their way of life was **characteristic**, or typical, of Indian civilizations before them. However, the discoveries at the Great Temple turned up new information about the Aztecs' religion, government, and other **cultural** features.

Objects found inside the temple are highly **descriptive** and show how the Aztecs worshiped. Some artifacts with **engravings**, or pictures etched on them, were put into special boxes. Archaeologists believe the careful way these boxes were preserved indicates that they were meant as offerings to gods. The **frequency** with which certain natural objects were found gives other hints to the nature of the Aztec religion. The great number of seashells, coral, and fish bones, for instance, suggests that these were offerings made to the gods of rain and water.

Scientists can also learn the exact size of the Aztec empire by determining where objects found in the temple came from. For example, three hundred stone masks found in the temple had been brought there by faraway peoples who lived under Aztec rule.

The contents of the Great Temple reflect the Aztecs' respect for the powers of nature. This **reverence** connects the Aztecs with ancient peoples and confirms the **continuity** of civilization.

★ Go back to the story. Underline the words or sentences that give you a clue to the meaning of each **boldfaced** word. ★

CONTEXT CLUES

In each sentence below a word or phrase is underlined. Choose a word from the box to replace that word or phrase. Write the word on the line.

continuity	excavate	descriptive	bonanza
characteristic	reverence	frequency	engravings
archaeologists	cultural		

1. Scientists who study the ancient past are interested in people and how they lived. _____

2. They must have patience, for sometimes they will dig up vast areas of ground before finding a single relic. _____

3. Other times, they may be lucky and find many objects that are a source of great fortune in terms of providing information about the past. _____

4. Often objects will provide information about a people's activities that are related to customs, arts, and beliefs. _____

5. Scientists always hope to find objects that are typical of a particular people. _____

6. When an object is found with repeated occurrence, then scientists can be sure it is typical. _____

7. Objects that are able to tell about a people are the most valuable to scientists. _____

8. Also valuable are pictures that have been etched in stone or metal. _____

9. These pictures often show a people's deep respect for nature or for a particular god or hero. _____

10. They may also show signs of a condition of going on without stopping from the past to the present. _____

CHALLENGE YOURSELF

Name two traits that are characteristic of Americans.

_____   _____

ANALOGIES

An **analogy** compares two pairs of words. The relationship between the first pair of words is the same as the relationship between the second pair of words. For example: Quick is to fast as loud is to noisy. Or an analogy may show that one thing is a type or kind of another thing. For example: Diamond is to jewel as iron is to metal. Use the words in the box to complete the following analogies.

excavate	characteristic	archaeologists	continuity
reverence	engravings	bonanza	

1. Strange is to unusual as _____ is to typical.

2. Ruin is to misfortune as _____ is to fortune.

3. Admiration is to love as _____ is to respect.

4. Dentists are to doctors as _____ are to scientists.

5. Pull is to tug as _____ is to dig.

6. Oaks are to trees as _____ are to drawings.

7. Day is to night as _____ is to change.

CLOZE PARAGRAPH

Use the words in the box to complete the passage. Then reread the passage to be sure it makes sense.

cultural	frequency	descriptive
engravings	continuity	archaeologists

   In many places around the world, (1) _____ looking for the remains of ancient peoples have found cave paintings. Sometimes the pictures are painted on the walls and sometimes they are

(2) _____ that have been etched in stone. But no

matter how they are done, the paintings are (3) _____ of the way a group lived in ancient times. The paintings show gods and heroes. They also show holidays, ceremonies, and other important

parts of the (4) _____ life of the people. The old cave

paintings are discovered with (5) _____. Through

time, these paintings show that there is some (6) _____ in the way people express themselves.

GET WISE TO TESTS

Directions: Read each sentence carefully. Then choose the best answer to complete each sentence. Mark the space for the answer you have chosen.

 Tip This test will show you how well you understand the meaning of the words. Think about the meaning of the boldfaced word before you choose your answer.

1. When you **excavate** to find treasure, you _____ for it.
   (A) shop
   (B) chop
   (C) dig
   (D) bargain

2. A box with **engravings** has _____ etched in it.
   (A) liquids
   (B) jewels
   (C) pictures
   (D) stones

3. **Archaeologists** would be looking for old _____ from the past.
   (A) people
   (B) relics
   (C) moons
   (D) trees

4. A discovery that can be called a **bonanza** will make someone _____.
   (A) poor
   (B) rich
   (C) tired
   (D) wary

5. A **characteristic** trait is one that is _____.
   (A) unusual
   (B) frightening
   (C) dangerous
   (D) typical

6. A **descriptive** poem gives a _____ picture.
   (A) song
   (B) word
   (C) sad
   (D) long

7. To get **continuity** in your writing, you must _____ your thoughts.
   (A) connect
   (B) display
   (C) remove
   (D) ignore

8. In **reverence**, he _____ to the king.
   (A) waved
   (B) sprinted
   (C) sailed
   (D) bowed

9. A visit to a _____ could be called a **cultural** experience.
   (A) zoo
   (B) doctor
   (C) planetarium
   (D) museum

10. A person whom you see with **frequency** is someone you see _____.
    (A) a lot
    (B) seldom
    (C) occasionally
    (D) today

Review

1. **Urbanites** are people who live in the _____.
   (A) country
   (B) delta
   (C) city
   (D) beach

2. A country in **turmoil** would have _____.
   (A) disorder
   (B) presidents
   (C) celebrations
   (D) ceremonies

3. One problem that may occur after a country starts **industrializing** is _____.
   (A) disease
   (B) tardiness
   (C) teaching
   (D) pollution

4. When you view something in **retrospect**, you think about it _____.
   (A) before it happens
   (B) after it happens
   (C) as it happens
   (D) not at all

Imagine that a housing developer wants to build apartments in an area that archaeologists from a nearby college strongly believe is filled with objects from colonial times. The apartments the developer will build are needed in your area, but the construction might destroy valuable colonial artifacts.

Should the excavating proceed, or should it be delayed? Write a paragraph in which you try to persuade others of your point of view. First state your opinion. Then give precise facts that back up your opinion. Use some vocabulary words in your writing.

Turn to "My Personal Word List" on page 131. Write some words from the story or other words that you would like to know more about. Use a dictionary to find the meanings.

★ Read the story below. Think about the meanings of the **boldfaced** words. ★

A New Peace

The first American soldier killed in Vietnam died in 1959. The last one died in 1975. During that sixteen-year period more than fifty thousand Americans lost their lives in combat. The conflict in Vietnam was not a popular war. Many Americans believed that the United States should never have sent soldiers to Vietnam and thought we should simply try to forget the war.

Some **veterans** of the war did not agree. For years they worked to have a monument built that would remind people of the **heroism** of those who had fought bravely and died. The veterans formed an organization and collected donations for the project from more than 275,000 people.

The group **authorized** a panel of art experts to find a designer. The panel, in turn, used its authority to announce a contest to consider artists' suggestions for the design of the memorial. All artists — painters, sculptors, and designers — were **eligible** to enter. It was to be a test of **creativity** to see who would come up with the most imaginative idea.

The panel received thousands of entries. The winning design came from Maya Ying Lin, a twenty-one-year-old student at Yale University. Lin wanted someday to design buildings, so she was studying **architecture**.

One of Lin's teachers helped her design the memorial. They combined their creative efforts to emphasize how important these lost lives were to the nation. They wanted to stress the idea that every single person was owed honor and respect. The memorial **dignifies** soldiers who gave their lives in battle.

The **completion** of the monument also marked the end of an era. There was less disagreement about the Vietnam War. The memorial seemed to bring people together in their sadness over the dead. The finishing of the memorial conceived by Maya Ying Lin was a **milestone** that marked an important moment in American history.

More than fifty thousand names appear on the Vietnam War Memorial. Each name represents an individual who died during the war. Some people say that the memorial gives these soldiers, in a sense, eternal life. The dead have won **immortality** by having their names carved into its face.

★ Go back to the story. Underline the words or sentences that give you a clue to the meaning of each **boldfaced** word. ★

USING CONTEXT

Meanings for the vocabulary words are given below. Go back to the story and read each sentence that contains a vocabulary word. If you still cannot tell the meaning, look for clues in the sentences that come before and after the one with the vocabulary word. Write each word in front of its meaning.

heroism	completion	eligible	creativity
veterans	authorized	immortality	architecture
dignifies	milestone		

1. _____ : makes noble or worthy

2. _____ : condition of being finished

3. _____ : those who have served in the armed forces

4. _____ : bravery, especially in a dangerous situation

5. _____ : the state of living forever

6. _____ : the planning and designing of buildings

7. _____ : gave power to

8. _____ : an important event

9. _____ : qualified; fit to be chosen

10. _____ : imagination; the ability to invent

CHALLENGE YOURSELF

Name two milestones in the history of the United States.

_____   _____

Name two people from history or literature who showed heroism.

_____   _____

Name two kinds of jobs that require a lot of creativity.

_____   _____

Name two buildings or monuments that you admire for their architecture.

_____   _____

WORD GROUPS

As you read each pair of words, think about how they are alike. Write the word from the box that best completes each group.

creativity	architecture	authorized	veterans
milestone	eligible	heroism	dignifies

1. bravery, courage, _____

2. enabled, allowed, _____

3. soldiers, sailors, _____

4. respects, honors, _____

5. suitable, acceptable, _____

6. cleverness, imagination, _____

7. building, design, _____

8. landmark, celebration, _____

WORD PAIRS

Words with similar parts may have related meanings. Study each word pair. Think about how the meanings are alike. Check the meanings in the Dictionary. Then write a sentence for each word.

1. **creation – creativity**

_____

_____

2. **heroic – heroism**

_____

_____

3. **dignity – dignify**

_____

_____

4. **authorize – authorization**

_____

_____

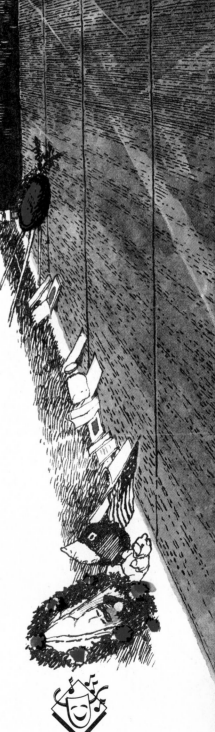

WORD MAP

Use the words in the box to complete the word map about the Vietnam War Memorial. Add other words that you know to each group. One heading will not contain any vocabulary words, only your words.

heroism	creativity	authorized
veterans	immortality	eligible

**What the Designer
Had to Be or Have**

1. _____

2. _____

3. _____

4. _____

5. _____

**What the Memorial
Stands For**

1. _____

2. _____

3. _____

4. _____

5. _____

VIETNAM WAR MEMORIAL

**Who Visits
the Memorial**

1. _____

2. _____

3. _____

4. _____

5. _____

**How Visitors Seeing
the Memorial Feel**

1. _____

2. _____

3. _____

4. _____

5. _____

GET WISE TO TESTS

Directions: Choose the word that best takes the place of the boldfaced word.

 Tip Some tests have letters inside the answer circles. Fill in the whole circle next to your answer, covering the letter, too.

1. The firefighter was decorated for **heroism**. He saved a child.
   A speed
   B bravery
   C luck
   D humor

2. He worked to save the whales. The plaque **dignifies** his efforts.
   A illustrates
   B aids
   C understands
   D honors

3. The **completion** of the project made them happy. Their work was done.
   A finishing
   B idea
   C category
   D organization

4. Winning the award was a major **milestone** in his life. Now he can go on to college.
   A fortune
   B help
   C event
   D intelligence

5. No human being has ever achieved **immortality**. Everyone dies eventually.
   A knowledge
   B interest
   C reason
   D everlasting life

6. She lived in the state. That made her **eligible** to vote there.
   A attractive
   B qualified
   C harmless
   D ignorant

7. The **architecture** of City Hall is stunning. It was built to display power.
   A design
   B politics
   C decoration
   D value

8. The **veterans** led the parade. It honored war heroes.
   A musicians
   B floats
   C former soldiers
   D former fathers

9. The voters **authorized** the mayor to stay in office. They did it by re-electing her.
   A welcomed
   B gave ideas to
   C placed blame on
   D gave power to

10. Her writing shows **creativity**. She amuses us with her fantastic stories.
    A imagination
    B loneliness
    C jealousy
    D happiness

Review

1. The tunnel will go through a mountain. They will **excavate** tons of earth.
   A transport
   B examine
   C dig out
   D unload

2. It was **characteristic** of her to be late. We never worried when she was tardy.
   A unusual
   B typical
   C troubling
   D strange

3. **Engravings** were on the walls. They were carved centuries ago.
   A Etchings
   B Buildings
   C Rules
   D Statues

4. They approached their hero with **reverence**. They felt in awe of him.
   A caution
   B deep respect
   C deep anger
   D demands

Think about the great sums of money needed to build a war memorial. Some people feel that the same money could be used to honor soldiers in another way. Do you agree or disagree?

Write a paragraph expressing your opinion about the best way to show respect toward those who have fought in wars. Use some vocabulary words in your writing.

_____

_____

_____

_____

_____

_____

_____

_____

_____

_____

_____

_____

_____

_____

_____

_____

_____

_____

_____

Turn to "My Personal Word List" on page 131. Write some words from the story or other words that you would like to know more about. Use a dictionary to find the meanings.

★ To review the words in Lessons 5–8, turn to page 126. ★

THE EARTH IS MOVING!

Usually, we are unaware of the earth's inner movements. However, a volcano or an earthquake graphically displays the results of motion taking place deep within the earth.

In Lessons 9–12, you will read about natural events that move the earth. Both earthquakes and volcanic eruptions can do a great deal of harm, especially in populated areas. What other natural events can cause disasters? How would you describe these events? Write your ideas under the headings below.

Natural Disasters

About Disasters

★ Read the story below. Think about the meanings of the **boldfaced** words. ★

CONTINENT   OCEAN

MANTLE

Quake, Tremble, and Roll

An earthquake sends no warning. It is one of nature's terrifying surprises. It begins with a **tremor**, a shaking, rolling motion underfoot. It might even be mistaken for the rumbling of a truck. During the next few seconds, buildings sway and windows shatter, disturbed by the sudden shock to the earth's surface.

Scientists say there may be as many as a million earthquakes in a single year. Most of them are not **destructive** and cause no damage. However, the **severity** of others is much greater. Earthquakes can set whole cities on fire, bring buildings crashing down, and cause many deaths.

Scientists have a theory involving plates that explains why earthquakes happen. According to this theory, there are a number of huge plates, or great rigid masses, under the earth's crust. These plates are in slow but continuous motion. They travel about one-half inch to four inches a year. Because the plates are not traveling in the same direction, sometimes two of them collide. When that happens, they **exert** pressure against each other, creating **friction**. Friction produces strain on the rocks at the plate's edge. At the **crucial** moment that the strain becomes too great, a sudden break occurs. It causes shock waves that move in all directions. The shock waves reach the surface, and the earth begins to shake and tremble.

The movement of the plates is also responsible for the creation of some mountains. When one plate is forced upward by another plate, it **disrupts** the earth above, tearing it apart. The earth that is pushed upward becomes a new mountain.

The plates do not have the same outlines as landmasses on earth. Each plate goes beyond the **contour** of the continents, out underneath the oceans. In fact, the plates cannot even be identified with a specific **hemisphere**, or half of the globe. In other words, the plates have shapes and movements all their own. They move under the earth's crust year after year. Yet these movements are not **audible** to the human ear. It is only when we hear the commotion created by an earthquake, feel the tremors, and see the destruction that we are reminded of the presence of the plates.

★ Go back to the story. Underline the words or sentences that give you a clue to the meaning of each **boldfaced** word. ★

CONTEXT CLUES

Read each pair of sentences. Look for clues to help you complete one of the sentences with a word from the box. Write the word on the line.

destructive	audible	crucial	tremor
severity	disrupts	contour	exert
friction	hemisphere		

1. Near dawn on April 18, 1906, certain plates underneath San Francisco began rubbing together. This _____ was so powerful that it caused the land above to split open.

2. As it began below the crust of the earth, the earthquake was silent. But moments later, the sounds of windows breaking and buildings falling were _____.

3. Cliffs fell into the ocean, and mountains filled small valleys. The _____ of the land changed for hundreds of miles all around.

4. The people of San Francisco were not aware that morning of the rolling and shaking far beneath their homes. When the strongest _____ hit the city, most people were still asleep.

5. The quake was strong enough to cause tremendous damage. Its _____ was such that the city hall collapsed into a pile of stone and brick, leaving only the frame standing.

6. Trains and trolleys and gas and water service were all stopped. A disaster like this _____ many public services.

7. Gas leaks caused fires, but water would not flow from fire hydrants because the water pipes had broken, too. It was _____ that water be found somewhere.

8. Fire raged for four days and destroyed 28,000 buildings in San Francisco. This frightening fact shows just how _____ a major earthquake can be.

9. Earthquakes can happen anywhere. Several of the most deadly have occurred in cities in the western _____.

10. Earthquakes _____ great pressure on tall buildings. Architects are trying to design buildings that will remain standing during a major quake.

REWRITING SENTENCES

Rewrite each sentence using one of the vocabulary words from the box.

exert	tremor	friction
hemisphere	contour	

1. This half of the earth has active earthquake areas.

   _____

2. The outline of a shore can be changed by an earthquake.

   _____

3. We felt the first shaking, rolling motion.

   _____

4. The rubbing of the giant plates was building rapidly.

   _____

5. The plates put pressure on one another.

   _____

CONNOTATIONS

Some words are very close in meaning, yet there is a small difference between them. The words suggest slightly different things. Remember that this means the words have different **connotations**. Read each sentence below. Choose a word in the box that has a slightly different connotation from the underlined word. Write the vocabulary word on the line.

crucial	destructive	disrupts	severity

1. An earthquake can be <u>harmful</u> to a whole city. _____

2. An earthquake's <u>harshness</u> determines how much damage is done. _____

3. It is <u>important</u> that every city have a disaster plan. _____

4. An earthquake <u>interrupts</u> many needed services. _____

TANGLED-UP WORDS

In the following passage, the underlined words do not make sense. But they sound similar to a word in the box. Study the context in which the underlined words appear. For each word, find the word in the box that should be used in its place. Write the correct word on the numbered line.

hemisphere	destructive	crucial	audible
friction	disrupted	exert	severity
tremor	contour		

Last summer my family decided to vacation in California. What a mistake! We arrived just in time for an earthquake!

Actually, we didn't even know an earthquake was occurring at first. We felt a (1) tractor, but we thought the shaking was from all the trucks passing outside. (We had begged to stay by the ocean, where the sound of the waves would be (2) edible, but instead we were by a freeway.) Then a jolt of greater (3) serenity hit. I was doing so much rolling and shaking, I felt like the left (4) atmosphere of my brain had traded places with the right!

About this time my father decided it was (5) cruelty for us to find a shelter where we would be safer. I was so afraid, I had to (6) exit all my strength just to make myself walk. I was sure that when we got outside, there would be fallen buildings, great holes in the earth, and other signs of the (7) decorative power of this earthquake.

What a shock! There was hardly any damage. Where I had expected the (8) contest of the land to have been altered violently, it looked just the same as when we arrived. We asked the motel owner if he was concerned, but he said this earthquake was just a minor one. "Just a little (9) fiction between the plates!" he laughed.

Well, two jolts in one day was enough for my family! We might seem like Eastern dudes from the days of the old West, but we checked out of that motel, climbed in our car, and headed for quiet ground. That earthquake may not have disturbed the natives, but it sure (10) erupted our vacation!

1. _____

2. _____

3. _____

4. _____

5. _____

6. _____

7. _____

8. _____

9. _____

10. _____

GET WISE TO TESTS

Directions: Read the sentence or sentences. Look for the best word to use in the blank. Mark the answer space for your choice.

 Tip Be sure to mark the answer space correctly. Do <u>not</u> mark the circle with an X or with a checkmark (✓). Instead, fill in the circle neatly and completely with your pencil.

1. The wildfire burned acres of forest and homes. The fire was very _____.
   - (A) helpful
   - (B) crucial
   - (C) destructive
   - (D) inferior

2. Janice had an acute pain in her side. She had to go to the doctor because of its _____.
   - (A) motion
   - (B) tremor
   - (C) weight
   - (D) severity

3. The explosion caused the house to shake. One wall cracked from this _____.
   - (A) tremor
   - (B) paint
   - (C) hemisphere
   - (D) sound

4. My father wants me to play football. He will _____ pressure on me to try out for the team.
   - (A) excel
   - (B) feel
   - (C) disrupt
   - (D) exert

5. This road follows the shoreline. We can see the _____ of the coast ahead.
   - (A) tremor
   - (B) city
   - (C) contour
   - (D) lighting

6. When my Uncle Fred visits, he wants to go places. He is fun, but he _____ our routine.
   - (A) prolongs
   - (B) disrupts
   - (C) disappoints
   - (D) exerts

7. Most of South America is below the equator. It is in the southern _____.
   - (A) hemisphere
   - (B) atmosphere
   - (C) friction
   - (D) district

8. The plates below the earth may rub against each other. This _____ can cause an earthquake.
   - (A) ripple
   - (B) contest
   - (C) friction
   - (D) hemisphere

9. If Jim wants to make the Olympic team, he must win the race. This is a _____ win for his career.
   - (A) modern
   - (B) unusual
   - (C) destructive
   - (D) crucial

10. The music was very soft, but it was still _____ to me.
    - (A) serious
    - (B) audible
    - (C) silky
    - (D) crucial

Review

1. During the war, he performed many brave deeds. Later, he received medals for his _____.
   - (A) fears
   - (B) fights
   - (C) immortality
   - (D) heroism

2. He wanted to enter the contest, but then he found out he was not _____. He was too young.
   - (A) pictured
   - (B) happy
   - (C) eligible
   - (D) childish

Imagine that a magazine has hired you to write about your experiences during a disaster. Think of a personal or natural disaster you have experienced or one that you have imagined.

Write an article about your experiences. Tell when each event happened and how you and others dealt with emergencies and fears. Use clue words such as <u>first</u>, <u>then</u>, and <u>finally</u> to keep the sequence clear. Use some vocabulary words in your writing.

Turn to "My Personal Word List" on page 132. Write some words from the story or other words that you would like to know more about. Use a dictionary to find the meanings.

★ Read the story below. Think about the meanings of the **boldfaced** words. ★

The Shark Callers

Near Australia lies the island of New Britain and the town of Rabaul. Andy Thompson and his family are visiting Rabaul when they learn that Matupi, one of the island's volcanoes, is about to erupt. Late at night, the Thompsons sail away from the island on board their boat, *Quintana*. By the next morning, they are sixty miles from Rabaul. The sea is calm and quiet, and it is Andy's turn at the wheel.

Andy decided to hoist the mainsail. It would help the engine out a bit and might add a knot to their speed.

He fastened the wheel and let *Quintana* look after herself while he put the sail up. It took only a few minutes to **winch** it into place. It flapped a little **halfheartedly** at first but eventually filled. It wouldn't make much difference, but at least it was something.

That, then, is how things stood when it happened.

At 8:37 the technicians at the Rabaul Vulcanological Institute noticed that the seismograph needles had begun to thrash dementedly up and down on their graph papers.

In the next forty seconds a small part of the world's map changed.

During the night a huge pressure point had been building deep beneath the waters of Rabaul Harbor. Seething lava and immense clouds of gases had pushed the thin crust of the harbor floor upward until a huge, bulbous abscess had formed.

At 8:37 exactly, the abscess **ruptured**. Lava spilled out into the water and sulfurous gas rocketed up from the depths, screaming out through the surface of the sea in a great blast of heat.

In the first twenty seconds a crack two miles long and half a mile wide tore the seabed open.

And in the next twenty seconds a billion gallons of water began to drain into it. Roaring in tremendous torrents, it hurtled down the white-hot channels and fissures, screamed through passages and tunnels, deep into the molten heart of the earth. Instantly vaporizing, the water became huge clouds of pressurized, superheated steam that rolled and crashed with hurricane force throughout the bubbling lava fields.

Here and there the water tumbling onto the lava cooled it, so that it solidified and closed exits where the pressure might have escaped; so pressure built elsewhere as steam, **mingled** with one-thousand-degree-centigrade gases, roared through further channels, seeking escape.

At 8:37 and forty seconds the earth could stand no more. The miles of underground channels pulsated and heaved under the strain as the huge gas clouds forced their arteries to the breaking point.

At that precise moment the entire end of the island, fifty square miles of land, with all it contained, ripped itself apart.

Rabalankaia, long **dormant**, vanished first. Great creaks appeared briefly in its sides and it exploded into a million pieces.

Impacted lava, squeezed through a thousand underground passages, **coursed** through the ground and found release through South Daughter, who lurched and shuddered briefly as though a vast fist pushed her up from somewhere deep in the ground. Then she, too, blew herself apart, her body **fragmented** into a cloud of rock and earth, hurled miles into the air with the ease of a child throwing up a handful of pebbles.

Rabaul, sitting in the apex of the caldera, stood no chance. A gigantic hand seemed to grip the entire town and crumple it. Twenty thousand homes, the huge shipping wharf, and the oceangoing ships **moored** at it simply began to sink into the mountainside, sucked in by the heaving earth. Then it was all spat out again as a torrent of lava spewed up from the depths of the volcano. Whole houses, incandescent with heat, sailed through the air like meteors, terrible, unearthly shooting stars arcing into the sky and dropping, sizzling, into the waters of the harbor.

For miles inland nothing survived. A great *nuee ardente*, a murderous blast of sulfurous gas and white-hot particles, tore out of the side of shattered Matupi and cut a swath of fiery devastation two miles wide across the land. Whole villages were incinerated, the people in them instantaneously carbonized. One second they were there; the next, all that remained of them was **smoldering** ash.

And, finally, ruined Matupi, writhing in its death throes, gave out its last cry.

A huge column of fire and smoke rocketed skyward into the atmosphere, where it began to spread and **obliterate** the sun.

The final release had been found.

Forty seconds and the world was forever changed.

The Gazelle Peninsula, with its hundred villages, its schools, its hospitals, its plantations and forests, was gone.

Rabaul was gone.

And in numbers no one would ever be able to count, the people were gone.

All gone.

In forty seconds.

From The Shark Callers, by Eric Campbell

★ Go back to the story. Underline any words or sentences that give you clues to the meanings of the **boldfaced** words. ★

USING CONTEXT

Meanings for the vocabulary words are given below. Go back to the story and read each sentence that has a vocabulary word. If you still cannot tell the meaning, look for clues in the sentences that come before and after the one with the vocabulary word. Write each word in front of its meaning.

mingled	coursed	dormant	halfheartedly
smoldering	ruptured	moored	fragmented
winch	obliterate		

1. _____: fastened in place with ropes or anchors

2. _____: to raise by using a machine for pulling

3. _____: to hide; to blot out

4. _____: without enthusiasm

5. _____: mixed together

6. _____: burst

7. _____: broken into pieces

8. _____: inactive

9. _____: moved quickly

10. _____: burning with little or no flame

CHALLENGE YOURSELF

Name two things that can be fragmented.

_____   _____

Name two things that could be smoldering.

_____   _____

Name two things you might do halfheartedly.

_____   _____

Name two things that can be dormant.

_____   _____

WORD GROUPS

Read each pair of words. Think about how they are alike. Write the word from the box that best completes each group.

ruptured	mingled	fragmented	dormant	winch
dormant	coursed	obliterate	moored	smoldering

1. smashed, splintered, _____

2. ran, flowed, _____

3. burning, smoking, _____

4. popped, burst, _____

5. hoist, elevate, _____

6. turned off, resting, _____

7. blended, mixed, _____

8. secured, fastened, _____

9. sleeping, inactive, _____

10. erase, devastate, _____

ANTONYMS

Remember that **antonyms** are words with opposite meanings. Match the words in the box with their antonyms listed below. Write each word on the line.

dormant	moored	halfheartedly
obliterate	mingled	fragmented

1. enthusiastically _____

2. to reveal _____

3. active _____

4. whole _____

5. adrift _____

6. separated _____

GET WISE TO TESTS

Directions: Read each sentence. Pick the word that best completes the sentence. Mark the answer space for the word.

Tip

If you are not sure which word best completes the sentence, do the best you can. Try to choose the answer that makes the most sense.

Review

1. The fate of the company will be decided at a _____ meeting next week.
   (A) lengthen
   (B) respecting
   (C) despair
   (D) crucial

2. To get the suitcase closed he had to _____ a lot of pressure.
   (A) lid
   (B) exert
   (C) clothes
   (D) acclaim

3. Only the cellar was left after the _____ floods.
   (A) destructive
   (B) water
   (C) ignition
   (D) only

4. The United States is in the northern _____.
   (A) southern
   (B) hemisphere
   (C) healthy
   (D) exploring

5. Whenever she sees a snake, her body shakes with a _____.
   (A) tremor
   (B) snowing
   (C) escaped
   (D) frosty

1. The _____ volcano had not exploded for hundreds of years.
   (A) moored
   (B) silly
   (C) dormant
   (D) dancing

2. The water _____ through the pipes with great speed.
   (A) trickled
   (B) coursed
   (C) mingled
   (D) coughed

3. During the eclipse, the moon will _____ the sun.
   (A) obliterate
   (B) love
   (C) reveal
   (D) behold

4. In the kitchen the smell of baking bread _____ with the aroma of roasting meat.
   (A) conspired
   (B) transmitted
   (C) simmered
   (D) mingled

5. I danced _____ because I didn't like the music.
   (A) forever
   (B) halfheartedly
   (C) happily
   (D) smoldering

6. The _____ clay pot could not be fixed.
   (A) mingled
   (B) noisy
   (C) fragmented
   (D) lunch

7. We must _____ the piano up to the second floor.
   (A) drop
   (B) obliterate
   (C) bounce
   (D) winch

8. When Kenzo squeezed the balloon, it _____.
   (A) ruptured
   (B) glowed
   (C) spoke
   (D) moored

9. We poured water on the _____ fire.
   (A) dead
   (B) halfheartedly
   (C) foreign
   (D) smoldering

10. The ships did not float away because they were _____ at the dock.
    (A) blue
    (B) moored
    (C) fragmented
    (D) wet

Writing

By sailing away on *Quintana*, Andy and his family escaped the eruption of Matupi. What do you think happened to the Thompsons next?

Pretend you are Andy, fleeing Rabaul with your family. Write a letter to a friend at home telling about some of your adventures after leaving New Britain. Think of specific events that might occur while you are at sea. Use some vocabulary words in your writing.

_____
                                          (Date)

Dear _____,

_____
_____
_____
_____
_____
_____
_____
_____
_____
_____
_____
_____
_____
_____
_____
_____
_____
_____
_____

Turn to "My Personal Word List" on page 132. Write some words from the story or other words that you would like to know more about. Use a dictionary to find the meanings.

★ Read the story below. Think about the meanings of the **boldfaced** words. ★

A Mountain of Surprises

Mount St. Helens was once 9,677 feet high, the fifth highest mountain in the state of Washington. On May 18, 1980, it **plummeted** to seventy-seventh place on the list of Washington's tallest peaks. What caused the change?

A volcano erupted inside the mountain. Red-hot ash and cinder shot out of its top. Large pieces of hot rock blasted high into the air. For eleven and a half hours, the mountain shook.

Then it was over. A smoky atmospheric haze hung in the sky over the mountain. The land for 12,000 square miles was buried under tons of rock, mud, and ash. Most of the mountain's **flora** and **fauna** — its plant and animal life — was destroyed. And the mountain itself had been **altered** forever, its top cut off like the top of a boiled egg.

Scientists said the situation was **disastrous**. They called Mount St. Helens a "dead-zone," a **blighted** place. They predicted it would take dozens of years before the mountain and the **adjoining** areas would be **livable**, and the animals would be able to return.

As it turned out, the scientists were wrong. Less than five years after the eruption, plant and animal life had returned to the mountain and its surroundings. Scientists were looking at **improbable**, hard-to-believe facts. But they could not argue with what they saw.

The first discovery was that some animals had survived. Insects and mammals that lived underground had been protected by the snow and earth covering them. Weeks after the eruption, these creatures came out of hiding. Scientists also learned that the wind carries more than five tons of dead insects to Mount St. Helens each summer. This heavy rain of insects acted as fertilizer for new plant life.

Next came another big surprise, the appearance of the Roosevelt elk. Scientists believed this animal could survive only in moist, thick forests. These elk were not expected to be able to **cope** with the blasted, barren slopes of Mount St. Helens. Yet there they were. Over 500 had returned to make the mountain their home! Mount St. Helens was indeed a mountain of surprises.

★ Go back to the story. Underline the words or sentences that give you a clue to the meaning of each **boldfaced** word. ★

CONTEXT CLUES

In each pair of sentences below, a word or phrase is underlined. Choose a word from the box to replace that word or phrase. Write the word on the line.

altered	improbable	flora	cope
blighted	plummeted	fauna	livable
adjoining	disastrous		

1. When Mount St. Helens erupted, <u>nearby</u> areas were greatly affected. All around, everything was covered with a thick layer of volcanic ash. _____

2. Ash landed on farms near the volcano. The <u>plants</u> wilted and died. _____

3. Many <u>animals</u> lived on the mountain. They were driven away for lack of food. _____

4. The damage to crops was great. Every farmer's profits <u>dropped quickly</u>, and farmers faced great hardship during that growing season. _____

5. The effect on the surrounding countryside was severe. You could see the <u>damaged</u> area extending over many miles in every direction. _____

6. The eruption <u>changed</u> the plans of a lot of people. Many had planned vacations on Mount St. Helens that had to be canceled. _____

7. People who lived in the area spent time doing <u>unlikely</u> household tasks. For example, it took days to shovel the ashes off roofs and gardens. _____

8. In time, people managed to clean up. Homes became <u>fit to live in</u> again. _____

9. The eruption was a big one. But it was not as <u>destructive</u> as it might have been. _____

10. People usually find a way to <u>deal</u> with problems. Even an erupting volcano was not too much for most people to handle.

_____

ANALOGIES

Remember that an **analogy** compares two pairs of words. The relationship between the first pair of words is the same as the relationship between the second pair of words. For example: <u>finger</u> is to <u>hand</u> as <u>toe</u> is to <u>foot</u>. Use the words in the box to complete the following analogies.

cope	adjoining	blighted	plummeted
fauna	flora	improbable	

1. Treat is to <u>injury</u> as _____ is to <u>problem</u>.

2. <u>Humorous</u> is to <u>funny</u> as _____ is to <u>unlikely</u>.

3. <u>Mineral</u> is to <u>calcium</u> as _____ is to <u>deer</u>.

4. <u>Soared</u> is to <u>upward</u> as _____ is to <u>downward</u>.

5. <u>Quick</u> is to <u>speedy</u> as _____ is to <u>neighboring</u>.

6. <u>Protected</u> is to <u>guarded</u> as _____ is to <u>destroyed</u>.

7. <u>Animal</u> is to <u>elephant</u> as _____ is to <u>daisy</u>.

WORD PAIRS

Words with similar parts may have related meanings. Study each word pair. Think about how the meanings of the words are alike. Check the meanings in the Dictionary. Then write a sentence for each word.

1. **disaster – disastrous**

_____

_____

2. **improbable – improbability**

_____

_____

3. **alter – alternate**

_____

_____

4. **live – livable**

_____

_____

GET WISE TO TESTS

Directions: Read each sentence carefully. Then choose the best answer to complete each sentence. Mark the space for the answer you have chosen.

 Tip Before you choose an answer, try reading the sentence with each answer choice. This will help you choose an answer that makes sense.

1. Something that has been **altered** has been _____.
   - (A) lost
   - (B) found
   - (C) allowed
   - (D) changed

2. A **disastrous** event causes _____.
   - (A) joy
   - (B) sadness
   - (C) contentment
   - (D) distance

3. A **blighted** place is _____.
   - (A) lively
   - (B) bright
   - (C) ruined
   - (D) active

4. A **livable** area is where animals make their _____.
   - (A) food
   - (B) living
   - (C) home
   - (D) lore

5. An **improbable** event is one that is _____ to happen.
   - (A) bearable
   - (B) unlikely
   - (C) likely
   - (D) mysterious

6. When you **cope** with a situation, you try to _____ it.
   - (A) ignore
   - (B) copy
   - (C) share
   - (D) handle

7. The **flora** of a region is its _____.
   - (A) folklore
   - (B) plant life
   - (C) animal life
   - (D) flood plain

8. A _____ might be one type of **fauna** in a region.
   - (A) maple tree
   - (B) farmer
   - (C) black bear
   - (D) black cloud

9. **Adjoining** homes are _____.
   - (A) expanded
   - (B) reflected
   - (C) adored
   - (D) nearby

10. The bird that **plummeted** to earth _____ quickly.
    - (A) dropped
    - (B) expanded
    - (C) rising
    - (D) plundered

Review

1. A picture that is **fragmented** is _____.
   - (A) artistic
   - (B) broken
   - (C) original
   - (D) new

2. To **winch** something is to _____ it.
   - (A) raise
   - (B) wrap
   - (C) lower
   - (D) describe

3. When a boat is **moored**, it is _____.
   - (A) antique
   - (B) drifting
   - (C) anchored
   - (D) broken

4. A **smoldering** fire is _____.
   - (A) loud
   - (B) newly made
   - (C) important
   - (D) burning slightly

Turn to "My Personal Word List" on page 132. Write some words from the story or other words that you would like to know more about. Use a dictionary to find the meanings.

Hundreds of newspapers reported the eruption of Mount St. Helens. People wanted to read all about it! Most newspaper stories answered the basic questions in the first paragraph: <u>What</u> happened? <u>Who</u> was affected by it? <u>When</u> did it happen? <u>Where</u> did it happen? <u>Why</u> did it happen? These five W's are the core of a first paragraph in a good newspaper report.

Think about an important or interesting event that has happened recently in your community or in your life. Write a paragraph that can serve as a first paragraph in a newspaper report about this event. Answer the five <u>W</u> questions. Use some vocabulary words in your writing.

★ Read the story below. Think about the meanings of
the **boldfaced** words. ★

How Big? How Serious?

An earthquake is always cause for concern. At the first sign of one, scientists begin to collect as much data as they can. How do they do it?

When an earthquake strikes, it sends out a pattern of shock waves. These waves, called **seismic** waves, move outward like ripples in a pond. Scientists use instruments that measure seismic waves. Within minutes, they know when an earthquake has released its **lethal** power. They also know exactly which areas are being affected by this deadly force.

However, for many years it was impossible to **evaluate** the power of an earthquake. Scientists had long tried, but their findings were **inadequate**. Without enough necessary information, their instruments could not be trusted.

Then, in 1935, Charles Richter announced the development of the Richter scale. The **accuracy** of this scale is absolute, always giving exact and true measurements. Richter was immediately recognized as an important **contributor** to the field of earthquake science.

Richter's scale is based on the movements of the earth. Special instruments measure ground motion. Then this information is used to **compute** a number. Each earthquake is given a number from 1 to 10 on the Richter scale. The number represents the severity of the quake. A Richter number of more than 5 means a serious quake. Earthquakes measuring a 7 or above on the scale can cause a great deal of damage. They can **devastate** an area.

Scientists cannot **avert**, or prevent, earthquakes. But they can **anticipate** when and where earthquakes might occur. For example, they have learned that when seismic waves sent out by large numbers of very small earthquakes start to slow down, a large earthquake may be about to take place.

With this information, scientists can then warn people in the threatened areas. Warnings provided by the Richter scale can help to save lives and to prevent some kinds of damage from occurring. In this way, Charles Richter's contribution was an important step in giving people some defense against earthquakes.

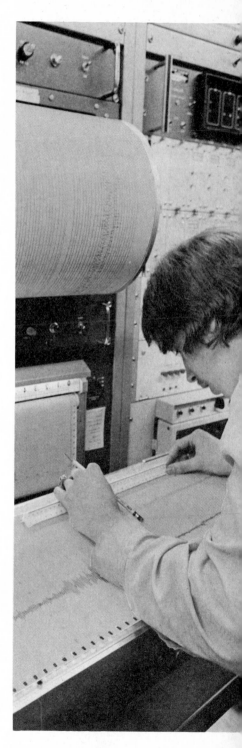

★ Go back to the story. Underline the words or sentences that give you
a clue to the meaning of each **boldfaced** word. ★

CONTEXT CLUES

Read each pair of sentences. Look for clues to help you complete one of the sentences with a word from the box. Write the word on the line.

devastate	evaluate	seismic	avert
anticipate	inadequate	lethal	accuracy
compute	contributor		

1. History is filled with stories of earthquakes. Until very recently, however, people had _____, or not enough, information about what caused them.

2. In 1755, an earthquake of _____ force struck the city of Lisbon, Portugal. Thousands of people died.

3. The heart of the city was destroyed. The citizens saw firsthand how an earthquake could _____ an area.

4. A man named John Mitchell made some studies after the Lisbon earthquake. In sharing what he learned, Mitchell became an early _____ to our knowledge of earthquakes.

5. Mitchell discovered that _____ waves, the waves from an earthquake, disturb everything in their path. This is why extremely large waves form in the ocean.

6. At first, people could only judge how serious an earthquake had been by comparing it to other earthquakes. To do this, they would _____ the destruction caused by each quake.

7. Looking at the wreckage left by an earthquake was not a precise way to measure its strength. A method whose _____ could not be questioned was needed.

8. Charles Richter knew that using mathematics would help people to measure accurately. He created a scale that scientists can use to _____ a number that tells how severe a quake is.

9. Increased knowledge of earthquakes has helped scientists learn how to predict when and where an earthquake may strike. Being able to _____ a quake has saved many lives.

10. People who live in earthquake areas have also learned how to prevent some kinds of damage from occurring. They have learned to _____ disaster by building stronger homes.

WORD GROUPS

As you read each pair of words, think about how they are alike. Write the word from the box that best completes each group.

compute	evaluate	lethal
devastate	contributor	anticipate

1. deadly, fatal, _____

2. ruin, destroy, _____

3. foresee, expect, _____

4. add, figure, _____

5. assistant, partner, _____

6. judge, estimate, _____

DICTIONARY SKILLS

Each numbered example has two parts. Answer the first part by writing a word from the box. Answer the second part by circling the correct choice. Use the **pronunciation key** in the Dictionary to help you when necessary.

accuracy	inadequate	avert
contributor	anticipate	

1. Write the correct spelling of in ad′i kwit. _____

   It means   **a.** more than is required   **b.** less than is required

2. Write the correct spelling of an tis′ə pāt′. _____

   It means   **a.** to see in advance   **b.** to be surprised

3. Write the correct spelling of kən trib′yə tər. _____

   It means   **a.** one who adds something   **b.** one who takes away

4. Write the correct spelling of ak′yər ə sē. _____

   It means   **a.** sloppiness   **b.** correctness

5. Write the correct spelling of ə vûrt′. _____

   It means   **a.** to hide from   **b.** to prevent

WORD GAME

The underlined letters in each sentence below are part of one of the vocabulary words. Use the underlined letters and the context of the sentence to determine the correct vocabulary word. Write the word on the line.

evaluate	contributor	seismic	averted
devastate	inadequate	accuracy	anticipate
compute	lethal		

1. The store placed an <u>ad</u> in the newspaper, but it wasn't enough to bring in new customers. _____

2. The cats sit by Meg's chair and look forward to a <u>pat</u> on the head. _____

3. That doctor has treated many athletes and has added to medical knowledge about how to treat a broken <u>rib</u>. _____

4. The hurricane could destroy all the crops in the <u>state</u>, which would ruin many farms and raise the prices of fruits and vegetables. _____

5. These chemicals and soaps could cause the death of a child, so please <u>let</u> me move them to a safer place. _____

6. I can believe <u>Cy</u> because his descriptions are almost always correct. _____

7. I think <u>it is</u> the shock waves that follow an earthquake that are the most frightening. _____

8. We <u>ate</u> dinner at a new restaurant, and after we thought about it, we decided it was one of the best meals we had ever eaten. _____

9. We have been studying the <u>Ute</u>, a tribe that lived in Utah, but we have not yet found out if they had a system for counting objects. _____

10. <u>Ted</u> turned his eyes away from the mess his baby brother had created on the kitchen floor. _____

Directions: Choose the word or words that best take the place of the boldfaced word. Mark your choice.

Tip Always read all the answer choices. Many choices may make sense. But only one answer choice has the same or almost the same meaning as the boldfaced word.

1. These essays are hard to **evaluate**. They present interesting facts, but are written poorly.
   - (A) recognize
   - (B) judge
   - (C) originate
   - (D) write

2. She was a **contributor** to that magazine. Several stories of hers were published in it.
   - (A) person who gave orders
   - (B) person who asked questions
   - (C) person who served food
   - (D) person who added something

3. A fire can **devastate** an area. Trees may be burned to ground level.
   - (A) invade
   - (B) destroy
   - (C) measure
   - (D) grow

4. George has a class in **seismic** studies. He is studying movements in the earth.
   - (A) universe
   - (B) math
   - (C) earthquake
   - (D) cells

5. Two minutes are **inadequate** for us to complete this test. We need more time than that.
   - (A) ample
   - (B) not enough
   - (C) very secret
   - (D) too much

6. The label warns these pills can be **lethal**. They could kill you.
   - (A) deadly
   - (B) rippling
   - (C) mild
   - (D) sick

7. He can **compute** in his head. He even does long division without pencil and paper.
   - (A) buy some books
   - (B) think about ideas
   - (C) figure out problems
   - (D) interest in movies

8. The weather forecaster said to **anticipate** rain today. A large storm is heading our way.
   - (A) wear
   - (B) force
   - (C) foresee
   - (D) suspect

9. The tire company was able to **avert** a strike. The owners agreed to what the workers wanted.
   - (A) prevent
   - (B) grant
   - (C) start
   - (D) offer

10. I doubt the **accuracy** of this scale. I know I weigh more than it indicates.
    - (A) secret
    - (B) warmth
    - (C) size
    - (D) correctness

Review

1. Please **convey** my message to your mother. It is very important that I meet with her.
   - (A) visit
   - (B) contact
   - (C) examine
   - (D) give

2. It is **improbable** that the rocket will land in our yard. It is aimed toward the ocean.
   - (A) usual
   - (B) impressive
   - (C) unlikely
   - (D) old-fashioned

Writing

After a major earthquake has occurred, television reporters are sent to the scene to find out what has happened. They usually try to interview people who have lived through the earthquake. They do this to try to get the most accurate and the most interesting information about the sequence of events.

Imagine that you are a reporter sent to cover a big earthquake. Write at least five questions that you will ask a person you might interview. Be sure to make your questions specific. Avoid questions that can be answered simply <u>yes</u> or <u>no</u>. Think of questions that require people to be descriptive when answering. Use some vocabulary words in your writing.

Turn to "My Personal Word List" on page 132. Write some words from the story or other words that you would like to know more about. Use a dictionary to find the meanings.

★ To review the words in Lessons 9–12, turn to page 127. ★

SENDING MESSAGES

Today we live in the age of information. The ability to communicate instantly with people all over the word brings everyone on our planet closer together.

In Lessons 13–16, you will read about different methods of communication. Imagine conversing by telephone with students in the Soviet Union, or using sign language to talk with someone who can't hear. Think about some of the different forms of communication we use. Why do we need to communicate? Write your ideas under the headings below.

Forms of Communication	**Reasons for Communicating**

★ Read the story below. Think about the meanings of the **boldfaced** words. ★

Ancient Symbols

Brightness

Sun

Moon

Writing with Symbols

Think of what our alphabet must look like to a five-year-old. There are 26 shapes, many of them very similar. It must be **bewildering**, leaving children puzzled and confused. Now imagine what a five-year-old in China has to face. The Chinese written language has no alphabet. It is made up of **characters**, or symbols, instead of letters. Each character represents an object or one or more ideas. Many characters look so much alike that they seem almost **identical**. Chinese has about 50,000 characters. To read a Chinese newspaper, you would need to know about 5,000 characters.

The Chinese written language is thousands of years old. At first, each character was a simple picture of what it represented. As the characters' meanings changed over time, they became more and more complex. For example, the character for the sun and the moon came to **signify**, or stand for, "brightness." "Sun" and "moon" are the **literal**, basic meanings of the character, while "brightness" is the **figurative** meaning of the two ideas together. A figurative meaning calls on your imagination, not just your understanding of single words.

For the Chinese, typewriters are **impractical**. A Chinese typewriter is difficult and slow to operate. It weighs 70 pounds, **excluding** the trays of characters that accompany it. If you include the weight of the trays, the machine weighs several hundred pounds. The Chinese prefer to write with a brush and ink.

Many Chinese people favor using the alphabet that we use. Such a change would make it easier for them to communicate with the world. Some Chinese people, however, view such a change as a threat to their traditions. They do not want foreigners **imposing**, or forcing, their customs on Chinese culture.

Another problem with using our alphabet is that our spelling is based on the sounds of words. This would create difficulty for the Chinese, for there are hundreds of **dialects** spoken throughout China. This means that different groups of people in different regions pronounce the same words differently. Imagine trying to spell when each pronunciation would be spelled in a different way!

★ Go back to the story. Underline the words or sentences that give you a clue to the meaning of each **boldfaced** word. ★

CONTEXT CLUES

In each sentence a word or phrase is underlined. Choose a word from the box that means the same as that word or phrase. Write the word on the line.

Modern Symbols

impractical	signify	imposing	characters
bewildering	literal	dialects	identical
figurative	Excluding		

1. In Chinese writing, many picture words have a meaning that is beyond the ordinary meaning. _____

2. Because there are more than 50,000 of these picture words, written Chinese can be confusing to an outsider. _____

3. Most Chinese marks and signs represent ideas. _____

4. One sign's actual meaning is "woman in a house." But this sign stands for the word "wife." _____

5. All Chinese can understand this sign, no matter what different forms of the spoken language they use. _____

6. If you are used to an alphabet, Chinese writing seems difficult to use, or ineffective. _____

7. The letters in an alphabet stand for sounds. _____

8. Not counting the fact that a letter may stand for different sounds, it is fairly easy to learn alphabet writing. _____

9. Some Chinese people worry about foreigners forcing their customs on China. _____

10. With an alphabet, these new words can be written with marks that are exactly alike. _____

Brightness

Sun

Moon

CHALLENGE YOURSELF

What is a figurative meaning of the word blue?

_____

WORD ORIGINS

Knowing the origin of a word can help you understand its meaning. Read each word origin. Then write each word from the box next to its origin.

signify	figurative	bewildering	characters
dialects	literal	identical	impractical

1. from Greek dialektos, conversation _____

2. from Latin idem, the same _____

3. from Old English wildernesse, wild place _____

4. from Latin signum, sign _____

5. from Latin littera, letter _____

6. from Greek praktos, to be done _____

7. from Latin figura, a form or shape _____

8. from Greek kharox, a pointed stake _____

MULTIPLE MEANINGS

Many words have multiple, or several, meanings. In a dictionary, each meaning of a word is numbered. You must decide which meaning fits the context.

Four meanings of character are given below. Look for clues in each sentence to tell which meaning is being used. Write the number of the meaning next to the correct sentence.

1. moral strength or weakness **2.** person or animal in a play, poem, or story **3.** letter, mark, or sign **4.** person who attracts attention by being different or odd

1. _____ There are thousands of written characters in Chinese.

2. _____ Their odd hairstyles make Bo and Mo real characters.

3. _____ Most of the characters in the book are realistic.

4. _____ The characters of heroes and cowards are different.

TANGLED-UP WORDS

In the following passage, the underlined words do not make sense. But they sound similar to a word in the box. Study the context in which the underlined words appear. For each word, find the word in the box that should be used in its place. Write the correct word on the numbered line.

bewildering	excluding	imposing	characters
literal	impractical	identical	figurative
signify	dialects		

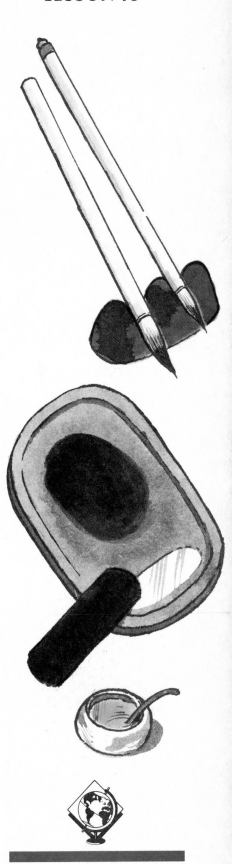

Last summer, my parents, my grandmother, and I visited relatives in Europe. Most of us had a confusing and (1) belonging time trying to make conversation. My relatives in Europe speak not only different languages, but also different (2) diapers. The members of my own family, (3) exciting my grandmother, speak only English. My grandmother had brought along some dictionaries telling what different foreign words (4) dignify. As we traveled along, she could quickly translate the (5) caretakers on signs. And here I had thought it was (6) impossible to pack such heavy books!

In Italy, we met Grandmother's (7) indefinite twin sister, my Great-Aunt Lucia. She welcomed us happily, so we didn't feel that we were (8) importing on her. However, when I said, "I've been dying to meet you!" Aunt Lucia understood only the (9) livable meaning of my words, and wanted to call a doctor. My grandmother had to explain to her that my expression was one of the many (10) furtive ones in English.

1. _____
2. _____
3. _____
4. _____
5. _____

6. _____
7. _____
8. _____
9. _____
10. _____

GET WISE TO TESTS

Directions: Read the sentences. Look for the best word to use in the blank. Mark the answer space for your choice.

Before you choose an answer, try reading the sentence with each answer choice. This will help you choose an answer that makes sense.

1. The washing machine costs $400. This is the price _____ the delivery charge, which is extra.
   - (A) excluding
   - (B) including
   - (C) bewildering
   - (D) sharing

2. It was difficult to tell the twins apart. They appeared to be _____.
   - (A) inevitable
   - (B) intelligent
   - (C) identical
   - (D) literal

3. The old car is still working. However, it uses so much gas that it is _____ to drive.
   - (A) figurative
   - (B) delightful
   - (C) impractical
   - (D) eligible

4. The poem is _____, for its message goes beyond the ordinary meaning of the words.
   - (A) hard
   - (B) literal
   - (C) figurative
   - (D) foolish

5. Let's vote on the proposal. All in favor of it, _____ your approval by raising your hand.
   - (A) signify
   - (B) hide
   - (C) cope
   - (D) enjoy

6. She is very democratic. She does not believe in _____ her ideas on others.
   - (A) needing
   - (B) using
   - (C) imposing
   - (D) excluding

7. The instructions are confusing. They are too _____ to follow.
   - (A) brief
   - (B) bewildering
   - (C) long
   - (D) figurative

8. He stated exactly what happened. He gave a very _____ account.
   - (A) literal
   - (B) false
   - (C) amusing
   - (D) excluding

9. The Chinese language has no alphabet. Instead it is made up of _____.
   - (A) sentences
   - (B) paragraphs
   - (C) pages
   - (D) characters

10. They all spoke the same language. But the language was made up of different _____.
    - (A) costumes
    - (B) flora
    - (C) values
    - (D) dialects

Review

1. The highway is covered with ice. We _____ that you will arrive late.
   - (A) avert
   - (B) neglect
   - (C) devastate
   - (D) anticipate

2. The judges observed the contestants. Then they would _____ the performances.
   - (A) evaluate
   - (B) convey
   - (C) compute
   - (D) emphasize

Chinese writing is made up of symbols. Many symbols stand for ideas. Think about five ideas that are important to you and write them on the lines at the left. Then think of a symbol to stand for each idea. Draw the symbols at the right.

Write a paragraph using your symbols each time you wish to state your idea. Your completed paragraph will consist of both symbols and words. Use some vocabulary words in your writing.

Ancient Symbols

Wife

	Ideas in Symbols
Ideas in Words	

1. _____   1.

2. _____   2.

3. _____   3.

4. _____   4.

5. _____   5.

Husband

_____

_____

_____

_____

_____

_____

Child

Turn to "My Personal Word List" on page 132. Write some words from the story or other words that you would like to know more about. Use a dictionary to find the meanings.

_____

_____

_____

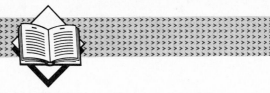

★ Read the story below. Think about the meanings of the **boldfaced** words. ★

The Story of My Life

Though unable to see, hear, or talk, Helen Keller learned to communicate and lead a fulfilling life. Here Helen Keller tells how a teacher, Anne Sullivan, led her to a miraculous breakthrough that changed her life.

THE MOST IMPORTANT DAY I remember in all my life is the one on which my teacher, Anne Mansfield Sullivan, came to me. I am filled with wonder when I consider the **immeasurable** contrasts between the two lives which it connects. It was the third of March, 1887, three months before I was seven years old.

On the afternoon of that **eventful** day, I stood on the porch, dumb, expectant. I guessed vaguely from my mother's signs and from the hurrying to and fro in the house that something unusual was about to happen, so I went to the door and waited on the steps. I did not know what the future held of marvel or surprise for me. Anger and **bitterness** had preyed upon me continually for weeks and a deep languor had succeeded this **passionate** struggle.

Have you ever been at sea in a dense fog, when it seemed as if a **tangible** white darkness shut you in, and the great ship, tense and anxious, groped her way toward the shore with plummet and sounding-line, and you waited with beating heart for something to happen? I was like that ship before my education began, only I was without compass or sounding-line and had no way of knowing how near the harbor was. "Light! give me light!" was the wordless cry of my soul, and the light of love shone on me in that very hour.

I felt approaching footsteps. I stretched out my hand as I supposed to my mother. Someone took it, and I was caught up and held close in the arms of her who had come to reveal all things to me, and, more than all things else, to love me.

The morning after my teacher came she led me into her room and gave me a doll. When I had played with it a little while, Miss Sullivan slowly spelled into my hand the word "d-o-l-l." I was at once interested in this finger play and tried to imitate it. When I finally succeeded in making the letters correctly, I was flushed with childish pleasure and pride. Running downstairs to my mother, I held up my hand and made the letters for doll. I did not know that I was spelling a word or even that words existed; I was simply making my fingers go in monkey-like imitation. In the days that followed, I learned to spell in this **uncomprehending** way a great many words, among them *pin, hat, cup* and a few verbs like *sit, stand,* and *walk*. But my teacher had been with me several weeks before I understood that everything has a name.

One day, while I was playing with my new doll, Miss Sullivan put a big rag doll into my lap also, spelled "d-o-l-l" and tried to make me understand that "d-o-l-l" applied to both. Earlier in the day we had had a **tussle** over the word "m-u-g" and "w-a-t-e-r." Miss Sullivan had tried to impress it upon me that "m-u-g" is *mug* and that "w-a-t-e-r" is *water*, but I persisted in confounding the two. In despair she had dropped the subject for the time, only to renew it at the first opportunity. I became impatient at her repeated attempts and, seizing the new doll, I dashed it upon the floor. I was keenly delighted when I felt the fragments of the broken doll at my feet. Neither sorrow nor regret followed my passionate **outburst**. I had not loved the doll. In the still, dark world in which I lived there was no strong **sentiment** of tenderness. I felt my teacher sweep the fragments to one side of the hearth, and I had a sense of satisfaction that the cause of my discomfort was removed. She brought me my hat, and I knew I was going out into the warm sunshine. This thought, if a wordless sensation may be called a thought, made me hop and skip with pleasure.

We walked down the path to the well-house, attracted by the fragrance of the honeysuckle with which it was covered. Some one was drawing water and my teacher placed my hand under the spout. As the cool stream gushed over one hand she spelled into the other the word *water*, first slowly, then rapidly. Suddenly I felt a misty consciousness as of something forgotten — a thrill of returning thought; and somehow the mystery of language was revealed to me. I knew then that "w-a-t-e-r" meant the wonderful cool something that was flowing over my hand. That living word awakened my soul, gave it light, hope, joy, set it free!

I left the well-house eager to learn. Everything had a name, and each name gave birth to a new thought. As we returned to the house every object which I touched seemed to quiver with life. That was because I saw everything with the strange, new sight that had come to me. On entering the door I remembered the doll I had broken. I felt my way to the hearth and picked up the pieces. I tried vainly to put them together. Then my eyes filled with tears; for I realized what I had done, and for the first time I felt **repentance** and sorrow.

From The Story of My Life, by Helen Keller

★ Go back to the story. Underline any words or sentences that give you clues to the meanings of the **boldfaced** words. ★

CONTEXT CLUES

Read each pair of sentences. Look for clues to help you complete one of the sentences with a word from the box. Write the word on the line.

bitterness	sentiment	uncomprehending	passionate
outburst	tangible	immeasurable	repentance
tussle	eventful		

1. Helen Keller's parents never gave up their efforts to help their

   daughter. They seemed to have _____ love and patience.

2. The Kellers' life began to improve when they hired Anne Sullivan. The young teacher's arrival marked the beginning of

   an _____ period in Helen's development.

3. Miss Sullivan had been blind when she was young and never fully

   recovered her eyesight. Rather than show any _____ from her childhood experiences, she was loving and eager to help.

4. Miss Sullivan was an extremely intense teacher. She had

   a _____ need to see Helen learn.

5. At first, Miss Sullivan had a difficult time working with Helen.

   They seemed to get into a _____ about everything.

6. Helen's parents believed their daughter knew little about the world. But Miss Sullivan sensed that Helen was not

   as _____ as she seemed.

7. When Helen had a fit of temper, her parents always gave in to her.

   Miss Sullivan met each _____ calmly and went on teaching.

8. Touching Helen's palm, Miss Sullivan traced the letters that spelled

   the names of things. This _____ spelling brought results.

9. In time, Helen was sorry for the difficulties she had caused her

   teacher. She expressed her _____ by hugging Miss Sullivan.

10. Miss Sullivan loved Helen. Added to this _____ was the one of pride in a job well done.

ANALOGIES

An **analogy** compares two pairs of words. The relationship between the first pair of words is the same as the relationship between the second pair of words. For example: <u>finger</u> is to <u>hand</u> as <u>toe</u> is to <u>foot</u>. Use the words in the box to complete the following analogies.

bitterness	eventful	tussle
tangible	passionate	

1. <u>Cold</u> is to <u>hot</u> as <u>uncaring</u> is to _____.

2. <u>Run</u> is to <u>race</u> as <u>fight</u> is to _____.

3. <u>Top</u> is to <u>bottom</u> as <u>sweetness</u> is to _____.

4. <u>Routine</u> is to <u>usual</u> as <u>holiday</u> is to _____.

5. <u>Color</u> is to <u>visible</u> as <u>softness</u> is to _____.

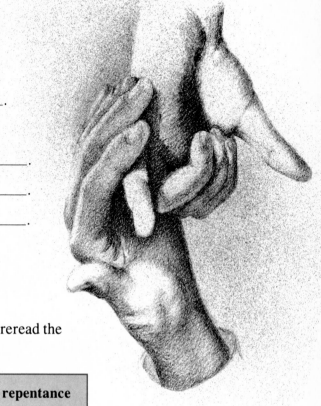

CLOZE PARAGRAPH

Use the words in the box to complete the paragraph. Then reread the paragraph to be sure it makes sense.

uncomprehending	immeasurable	tangible	repentance
outburst	sentiment	tussle	

In an (1) _____ of temper, Helen threw food on the floor. The child seemed (2) _____ about the proper way to behave at the table. But Miss Sullivan thought Helen was testing her family. She understood this (3) _____.

With (4) _____ calm, she put the food back on Helen's plate. Helen felt the food and threw it again. This was a

(5) _____ way of saying, "I dare you to make me eat it!" This (6) _____ with food went back and forth, but finally Helen gave in and ate her supper. Later she apologized, showing her (7) _____.

GET WISE TO TESTS

Directions: Read each sentence. Pick the word that best completes the sentence. Mark the answer space for the word.

 Some tests put letters before the answer choices. Be sure to find the letter of the answer you think is correct, then fill in the circle beside it.

Review

1. These marks _____ letters.
   A ○ likes
   B ○ signify
   C ○ sulphurous
   D ○ neatly

2. The sounds of a foreign language can be _____.
   A ○ strangely
   B ○ bewildering
   C ○ speak
   D ○ under

3. No two people's fingerprints are _____.
   A ○ press
   B ○ interest
   C ○ carefully
   D ○ identical

4. It costs ten dollars, _____ tax.
   A ○ excluding
   B ○ paid
   C ○ heavy
   D ○ their

5. You are _____ on me.
   A ○ comparatively
   B ○ happen
   C ○ imposing
   D ○ inquiry

---

1. His _____ showed when he lost the contest.
   A ○ tangible
   B ○ angrily
   C ○ needed
   D ○ bitterness

2. Tuesday was an _____ day at school.
   A ○ repentance
   B ○ enlighten
   C ○ eventful
   D ○ excite

3. The number of stars is _____.
   A ○ immeasurable
   B ○ passionate
   C ○ consider
   D ○ count

4. The sudden _____ broke the silence.
   A ○ eventful
   B ○ loudly
   C ○ outburst
   D ○ erupt

5. She apologized to me with _____.
   A ○ repentance
   B ○ uncomprehending
   C ○ attitude
   D ○ fearsome

6. There is strong _____ to save the whales.
   A ○ importantly
   B ○ emotional
   C ○ sentiment
   D ○ immeasurable

7. He stared at her in an _____ way.
   A ○ achievement
   B ○ uncomprehending
   C ○ understand
   D ○ eagerly

8. She expressed her ideas with _____ feeling.
   A ○ accomplishment
   B ○ artificially
   C ○ bitterness
   D ○ passionate

9. The fluffy clouds were so close to the ground that they seemed almost _____.
   A ○ tussle
   B ○ tangible
   C ○ clash
   D ○ nowhere

10. The hot-tempered children got into a _____.
    A ○ fights
    B ○ uncomprehending
    C ○ tussle
    D ○ legacy

Helen Keller was both blind and deaf. Think about your five senses (sight, hearing, smell, touch, and taste). Which one of these senses do you appreciate most?

Write a paragraph describing this sense. Tell how the use of the sense makes your world complete. Use some vocabulary words in your writing.

Turn to "My Personal Word List" on page 132. Write some words from the story or other words that you would like to know more about. Use a dictionary to find the meanings.

★ Read the story below. Think about the meanings of the **boldfaced** words. ★

A Smaller World

In October 1957, the first satellite, called *Sputnik*, was sent into orbit. Today, hundreds of satellites are spinning around Earth.

Communications satellites, sent up by the United States and other nations, are among the most important of these devices that revolve around Earth. In countless ways, these satellites have improved life for much of **humankind.** They have brought people together and made Earth a smaller place.

For Americans, watching an Olympic competition live from Norway was an **impossibility** just a few years ago. But today we can see an event that takes place almost anywhere in the world. From the clarity of the image, we cannot tell that the broadcast – in color and in focus – is coming from another continent thousands of miles away.

How does satellite communication work? Powerful devices send TV signals from the earth to the satellites. After a satellite picks up the TV signals, it beams them back to Earth over a wide area. These signals are received by special "dishes" on Earth. These dishes are electronic devices with large curved shapes that resemble a dish. They **transmit** the signals, sending them out to be picked up by your television set.

Modern satellites can transmit very strong signals. As a result, the devices that pick up these signals do not have to be very large. **Amazingly**, people can set up dishes that are small enough to fit on the roof of a house. These astonishing **contraptions** are called Direct Broadcasting Satellites.

In another way, communications satellites have increased our **closeness** to the rest of the world. Before the twentieth century, there was no such thing as an **overseas** telephone call. Instead, people sent letters and other **correspondence** across the oceans by ship. Today, communications satellites relay thousands of international phone calls at the same time. Americans can talk to friends and relatives on other continents, and their voices sound perfectly clear.

Communications satellites have far **exceeded** the dreams of the first pioneers who launched them. They do more than these pioneer scientists ever expected to make Earth a smaller world.

★ Go back to the story. Underline the words or sentences that give you a clue to the meaning of each **boldfaced** word. ★

USING CONTEXT

Meanings for the vocabulary words are given below. Go back to the story and read each sentence that contains a vocabulary word. If you still cannot tell the meaning, look for clues in the sentences that come before and after the one with the vocabulary word. Write each word in front of its meaning.

clarity	overseas	impossibility	amazingly
humankind	transmit	correspondence	contraptions
closeness	exceeded		

1. _____ : with wonder or astonishment; in a particularly surprising way

2. _____ : devices or gadgets

3. _____ : human beings; all people

4. _____ : clearness; state of being easily seen or understood

5. _____ : something that cannot be accomplished

6. _____ : across or beyond the sea; abroad

7. _____ : letters and other written messages

8. _____ : to send out by means of electronic waves

9. _____ : did more than; went beyond

10. _____ : a state of being near in some way

CHALLENGE YOURSELF

Name two countries you would travel overseas to visit.

_____   _____

Name two contraptions you might find in a kitchen.

_____   _____

Name two things that you think humankind needs most.

_____   _____

Name two things we are able to do today that would have been considered an impossibility a century ago.

_____   _____

ANTONYMS

In each sentence, one word is underlined. That word sounds silly in the sentence. Choose a word from the box that is an **antonym** of the silly word in the sentence. Write that word on the line.

impossibility	clarity	closeness
Amazingly	transmit	Overseas

1. _____: Through sharing their thoughts and feelings, the friends developed a real distance.

2. _____: Local telephone calls cost a great deal of money.

3. _____: He hoped to prove the possibility of time travel.

4. _____: Unsurprisingly, the magician vanished into thin air.

5. _____: The confusion of her report was impressive.

6. _____: A television studio can receive a broadcast anywhere in the area.

WRITING SENTENCES

Write an original sentence with each of the words in the box.

contraptions	humankind	exceeded	correspondence

1. _____

_____

2. _____

_____

3. _____

_____

4. _____

_____

Directions: Read each sentence carefully. Then choose the best answer to complete each sentence. Mark the space for the answer you have chosen.

 Tip Some tests have letters inside the answer circles. Fill in the circle next to your answer, covering the letter, too.

1. **Contraptions** are _____.
   - (A) jokes
   - (B) toys
   - (C) devices
   - (D) plans

2. When you go **overseas**, you travel _____.
   - (A) abroad
   - (B) near
   - (C) nearby
   - (D) quickly

3. An **amazingly** good movie is _____ delightful.
   - (A) particularly
   - (B) sadly
   - (C) less than
   - (D) not

4. A person who writes with **clarity** writes _____.
   - (A) quickly
   - (B) slowly
   - (C) humorously
   - (D) clearly

5. **Correspondence** usually is carried on through _____.
   - (A) songs
   - (B) letters
   - (C) stamps
   - (D) addresses

6. When you **transmit** something, you _____ it.
   - (A) fix
   - (B) borrow
   - (C) send
   - (D) throw

7. Something that benefits **humankind** helps _____.
   - (A) your friends only
   - (B) your community only
   - (C) plants and animals
   - (D) people everywhere

8. Something that is an **impossibility** is _____.
   - (A) sure to happen
   - (B) likely to happen
   - (C) easy to do
   - (D) not possible

9. Countries known for their **closeness** on the map are _____.
   - (A) near each other
   - (B) far apart
   - (C) unfriendly
   - (D) the same size

10. When he **exceeded** the speed limit, he _____.
    - (A) obeyed it
    - (B) discussed it
    - (C) went beyond it
    - (D) went under it

Review

1. An **eventful** day is full of _____.
   - (A) hours
   - (B) happenings
   - (C) children
   - (D) seconds

2. Something **tangible** can be _____.
   - (A) touched
   - (B) whispered
   - (C) spoken
   - (D) dreamed

3. If you feel **repentance**, you are _____.
   - (A) angry
   - (B) curious
   - (C) sorry
   - (D) sleepy

4. An **outburst** is a fit of _____.
   - (A) tears
   - (B) temper
   - (C) whispers
   - (D) cheers

5. **Passionate** feelings are ones you feel _____.
   - (A) slightly
   - (B) a little
   - (C) strongly
   - (D) coolly

6. Something that is **immeasurable** _____.
   - (A) cannot be counted
   - (B) cannot be seen
   - (C) can be counted
   - (D) can be measured

Writing

Think about a common communications device: the telephone. Imagine that you meet someone who has never heard of a telephone, much less used one.

Write a paragraph explaining what the telephone is used for. Then give step-by-step directions for placing a telephone call. Remember to keep the steps in sequence as you write them on the lines below. Use some vocabulary words in your writing.

Turn to "My Personal Word List" on page 132. Write some words from the story or other words that you would like to know more about. Use a dictionary to find the meanings.

★ Read the story below. Think about the meanings of the **boldfaced** words. ★

Many Talents, Many Faces

Millions of people have watched Hector Elizondo play the role of Dr. Phillip Watters on the television drama *Chicago Hope*. This **exposure** is welcomed by Elizondo. And finally, after years in the acting business, he is now recognized by name. Elizondo is grateful for his **involvement** in *Chicago Hope*. He is also pleased that the new **acceptance** gives him national recognition. At last, people recognize his name as well as his face.

Elizondo's fans now appreciate his wealth of talents. He can seemingly play any **ethnic** role, changing his voice as needed to reflect different nationalities and cultures. Among the different ethnic roles he has successfully played are a French police officer, a Jewish prosecuting attorney, a Swedish doctor, and an Asian chauffeur. Elizondo's **expressive** face and voice convince his audiences that he really is whatever character he plays. It seems easy for him to **evoke** responses of laughter, tears, or sympathy.

The son of parents from Puerto Rico, Elizondo was raised on the edge of Harlem in New York City. Among the neighbors on his block were African Americans, Italians, Irish, Japanese, and Finns. Far from being a **disadvantage**, this background has helped him adapt to his different roles. "Everything I do is something I remember from when I was a kid," Elizondo says. He explains that if he needs to sound Scandinavian, he just remembers a Finnish friend who was one of his buddies. A variety of youthful experiences helped Elizondo steadily develop his skills. They helped to **instill** in him many of the talents that an actor needs.

Elizondo's first major success came in 1970 when he portrayed a Puerto Rican service attendant in an off-Broadway play. After that, Elizondo was offered Hispanic parts in several popular productions. He refused most of them, however, because he did not want to be typecast in only Hispanic roles. Elizondo did not want his career to be **confined** in that way. He also wanted to take on **conventional** roles – traditional characters who might be played by any actor. Elizondo's insistence on playing diverse roles has made his career more challenging and much more rewarding. Now people applaud his many talents as well as his many faces.

★ Go back to the story. Underline the words or sentences that give you a clue to the meaning of each **boldfaced** word. ★

USING CONTEXT

Meanings for the vocabulary words are given below. Go back to the story and read each sentence that has a vocabulary word. If you still cannot tell the meaning, look for clues in the sentences that come before and after the one with the vocabulary word. Write each word in front of its meaning.

acceptance	involvement	instill	disadvantage
exposure	confined	evoke	conventional
expressive	ethnic		

1. _____ : usual, traditional

2. _____ : to teach little by little

3. _____ : being seen, being known

4. _____ : an unfavorable circumstance

5. _____ : the act of taking part

6. _____ : showing many emotions

7. _____ : approval

8. _____ : limited, held back

9. _____ : having to do with religious, racial, national, or cultural groups

10. _____ : to call forth, bring out

CHALLENGE YOURSELF

Name two ways of gaining the <u>acceptance</u> of your teacher.

_____   _____

Name two <u>conventional</u> ways of getting to school.

_____   _____

Name two ways of achieving <u>involvement</u> in the life of your community.

_____   _____

Name two ways a baseball team can <u>evoke</u> cheers from a crowd.

_____   _____

ANTONYMS

Remember that **antonyms** are words with opposite meanings. Match the words in the box with their antonyms listed below. Write each word on the line.

confined	instill	conventional	evoke
disadvantage	expressive	acceptance	

1. emotionless _____

2. benefit _____

3. free _____

4. rejection _____

5. unusual _____

6. suppress _____

7. erode _____

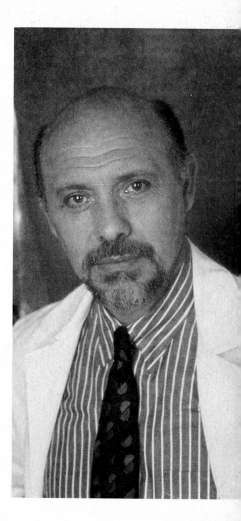

CLOZE PARAGRAPH

Use the words in the box to complete the paragraph. Then reread the paragraph to be sure it makes sense.

exposure	involvement	instill	ethnic
disadvantage	conventional		

Hector Elizondo grew up in a very diverse neighborhood in

New York City. His _____ to many different

_____ groups helped to _____
in him the ability to portray characters of many different cultures and
nationalities. Elizondo has never found his background to be a

_____, or obstacle. As a result, he has played

many _____ roles as well as nontraditional ones.

Elizondo's _____ in popular television shows has
made him well known to the public.

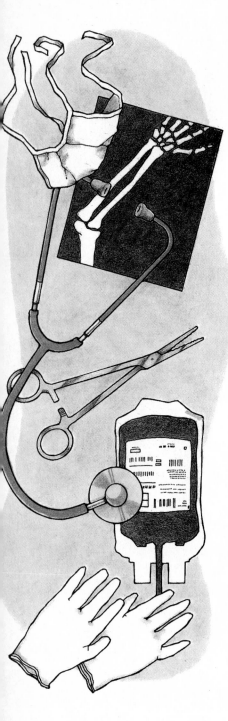

WORD ORIGINS

Knowing the origin of a word can help you understand its meaning. Read each word origin. Then write each word from the box next to its origin.

exposure	acceptance	instill
confined	evoke	ethnic

1. from the Latin *accipere*, to receive _____

2. from the French *exposer*, to expose _____

3. from the Latin *evocare*, to call forth _____

4. from the French *confin*, boundary _____

5. from the Latin *instillare*, to drip in _____

6. from the Greek *ethnikos*, of a national group _____

WRITING SENTENCES

Use each vocabulary word in the box to write an original sentence.

disadvantage	conventional	involvement
expressive	acceptance	exposure

1. _____

2. _____

3. _____

4. _____

5. _____

6. _____

Directions: Choose the word that best takes the place of the boldfaced word.

Tip

Always read all the answer choices. Many choices may make sense but only one answer choice has the same or almost the same meaning as the boldfaced word.

1. The cat is **confined** to the house. It is never allowed out.
   - (A) attached
   - (B) limited
   - (C) helped
   - (D) authorized

2. He gained our **acceptance**. So we asked him to join the club.
   - (A) hatred
   - (B) delight
   - (C) approval
   - (D) knowledge

3. This area of town has several **ethnic** restaurants. My favorite is the Japanese steak house.
   - (A) crowded
   - (B) filled with decorations
   - (C) expensive
   - (D) from different cultures

4. **Conventional** methods will not work. We must do something out of the ordinary.
   - (A) Traditional
   - (B) Unusual
   - (C) Exciting
   - (D) Brilliant

5. TV gives athletes much **exposure**. People recognize them at once.
   - (A) money
   - (B) joy
   - (C) notice
   - (D) work

6. The father wished to **instill** confidence in his children. Therefore he praised them often.
   - (A) prevent
   - (B) force
   - (C) gradually create
   - (D) suddenly stop

7. He told the judge that he had no **involvement** in the crime. He maintained he was miles away at the time.
   - (A) liking for
   - (B) part in
   - (C) solution to
   - (D) questions about

8. The actress was able to **evoke** tears from an audience. She moved everyone.
   - (A) bring forth
   - (B) put aside
   - (C) wipe
   - (D) flow

9. In some sports, being short may be a **disadvantage**. But you can make up for this with speed.
   - (A) drawback
   - (B) result
   - (C) improvement
   - (D) help

10. The child had very **expressive** eyes. One moment they were sad, the next moment they were joyful.
    - (A) deep
    - (B) colorful
    - (C) showing much feeling
    - (D) showing no feeling

Writing

Hector Elizondo has appeared in many motion pictures and has played many different kinds of characters. Think about your favorite character from a movie or television show. Is he or she very different from you? Would you like the chance to play your favorite character?

Write a paragraph about your favorite character. Describe him or her and explain why you would like to play that person. Use some vocabulary words in your writing.

_____

_____

_____

_____

_____

_____

_____

_____

_____

_____

_____

_____

_____

_____

_____

_____

_____

_____

_____

_____

_____

Turn to "My Personal Word List" on page 132. Write some words from the story or other words that you would like to know more about. Use a dictionary to find the meanings.

★ To review the words in Lessons 13–16, turn to page 128. ★

SPIRIT OF ADVENTURE

Mountain climbers, race-car drivers, underwater explorers, and airplane pilots have one thing in common. They all share a spirit of adventure!

In Lessons 17–20, you will read about some brave and adventurous people. Imagine climbing to the top of a majestic mountain or exploring the depths of the sea. Think about some jobs associated with adventure, excitement, and even danger. What qualities do you think a person doing such work would have? Write your ideas on the lines below.

Adventurous Work

Qualities of Adventurers

_____

_____

_____

_____

_____

_____

_____

_____

_____

_____

★ Read the story below. Think about the meanings of the **boldfaced** words. ★

Wonder Woman

Kitty O'Neil inches cautiously across the roof of an apartment building as a would-be killer forces her toward the edge. Suddenly, she slips and disappears over the side!

It's all in a day's work for Kitty O'Neil. She is a stuntwoman who makes her living doing hazardous tricks and **acrobatics** in the movies. In this scene she is taking the place of an actress who could not do these things. Dangerous scenes in movies are almost always performed by stuntpeople. During these scenes they assume the **identity** of the star. They wear the same clothing and hairstyle. They are matched so their height and weight are the same, too.

O'Neil first became interested in doing stunts when she married a stuntman, Duffy Hambleton. She asked him to teach her what he knew. Soon she was learning to fall, to fake fights, and to roll cars. Within a few years, she was a popular stuntwoman in Hollywood.

Being a successful stuntwoman requires great **coordination**. O'Neil must be in top form and able to move well. Even so, she wears a harness in stunts where she falls off a roof.

O'Neil does a lot of car and motorcycle stunts. During a chase scene in one movie, she rolled a car over three times. Such **antics** take plenty of physical skill and training. They also take great **agility**. But O'Neil can deliver. Her movements are quick and easy and right on target. Kitty O'Neil is an **ace**, tops in her field.

In her private life, O'Neil has known real **adversity**. When she was four months old, she got measles, mumps, and smallpox all at the same time. She had an alarmingly high fever, and no doctor was available to care for her. After several days, her temperature did come down, but the damage was done. O'Neil had lost her hearing.

O'Neil has never let this **disability** become an obstacle to achievement. In fact, she has always looked at her deafness as a challenge. Besides being a stuntwoman, Kitty O'Neil is also a race-car driver. She finds this sport exciting and **exhilarating**. She holds twenty-nine world speed records.

Kitty O'Neil doesn't see herself as Wonder Woman. But her **assurance** and confidence have helped her achieve many goals.

★ Go back to the story. Underline the words or sentences that give you a clue to the meaning of each **boldfaced** word. ★

CONTEXT CLUES

Read each pair of sentences. Look for clues to help you complete the second sentence with a word from the box. Write the word on the line.

identity	disability	antics	agility
acrobatics	coordination	ace	assurance
adversity	exhilarating		

1. Kitty O'Neil is deaf. But she has never let this

   _____ stop her from achieving her goals.

2. She performs hazardous stunts in the movies. She is very good at

   these _____.

3. O'Neil often takes the place of the leading actress. She assumes

   the _____ of that star while doing dangerous
   stunts.

4. A stunt person must be able to move with grace and balance. It

   takes _____ to avoid injury.

5. A good stunt person must be able to move quickly and easily while

   performing stunts. O'Neil has the _____ that is
   needed to be one of the best stuntwomen in the movies.

6. O'Neil also believes in herself and in her abilities.

   That _____ has contributed to her success.

7. Such qualities have helped O'Neil to face difficult trials in her life.

   She has not let _____ defeat her.

8. Instead, O'Neil strives to be the best at whatever she does. She is

   an _____ stuntwoman and a top race-car driver.

9. Rolling a car is deadly serious business to O'Neil. She does not

   consider such activities to be just pranks or _____.

10. Skilled people like Kitty O'Neil find excitement in racing a car at top

    speeds. They find the experience _____ because
    they are in control.

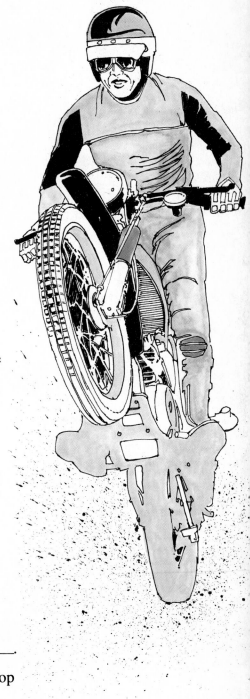

CONNOTATIONS

Some words are very close in meaning, yet there is a small difference between them. The words suggest slightly different things. This means the words have different **connotations**. Read each question below. Choose the underlined word that is the more appropriate answer to each question. Write the word on the line.

1. Who would perform a plane stunt with greater ease, a <u>master</u> or an <u>ace</u>? _____

2. Which is harder to overcome, an <u>adversity</u> or a <u>difficulty</u>? _____

3. Which actions — <u>tricks</u> or <u>antics</u> — are more likely to cause laughter? _____

4. Which would an Olympic gymnast do in a competition, <u>stunts</u> or <u>acrobatics</u>? _____

5. Which would be the better word to describe a trip in a hot-air balloon, <u>exhilarating</u> or <u>lively</u>? _____

6. Which would a criminal work hard to hide, his <u>identity</u> or his <u>appearance</u>? _____

WORD PAIRS

Words with similar parts may have related meanings. Study each word pair. Think about how the meanings of the words are alike. Check the meanings in the Dictionary. Then write a sentence for each word.

1. assure — assurance

   _____

   _____

2. disable — disability

   _____

   _____

3. agile — agility

   _____

   _____

WORD MAP

Use the vocabulary words in the box to complete the word map about stunt performers. Add other words that you know to each group.

| acrobatics | coordination | ace |
| agility | exhilarating | antics |

What Stunt Performers Do

1. _____
2. _____
3. _____
4. _____
5. _____

Qualities of Stunt Performers

1. _____
2. _____
3. _____
4. _____
5. _____

STUNT PERFORMERS

Terms that Describe Stunt Performers

1. _____
2. _____
3. _____
4. _____
5. _____

How Audiences Might Describe Stunt Performances

1. _____
2. _____
3. _____
4. _____
5. _____

GET WISE TO TESTS

Directions: Choose the word or words that best take the place of the boldfaced word.

Tip

This test shows how well you understand the meaning of the words. Think about the meaning of the boldfaced word before you choose your answer.

1. I loved the clown's **antics**. He was the funniest performer in the circus.
   - (A) outburst
   - (B) costume
   - (C) pranks
   - (D) props

2. Holly has a **disability** in school. She has difficulty reading.
   - (A) disadvantage
   - (B) headache
   - (C) trial
   - (D) blindness

3. A gymnast must have excellent **coordination**. It takes grace and skill to maintain such body control.
   - (A) harmonious movements
   - (B) concentration
   - (C) endurance
   - (D) excitement

4. She kept her **identity** a secret. She did not want people to ask her for her autograph.
   - (A) travel plans
   - (B) family relationships
   - (C) bank account
   - (D) name and appearance

5. I could watch the kittens jump and play for hours. Their **acrobatics** delight me.
   - (A) dialects
   - (B) gymnastic tricks
   - (C) methods of eating
   - (D) balls of yarn

6. This test will measure your **agility**. You must run the course and jump over objects of different heights.
   - (A) ability to plan races
   - (B) knowledge of colors
   - (C) quick and easy movements
   - (D) understanding and patience

7. Lionel entered the contest with a great deal of **assurance**. He felt sure he would win.
   - (A) acceptance
   - (B) involvement
   - (C) confidence
   - (D) wonderment

8. Carol is an **ace**. She can make an old engine work like a new one.
   - (A) expert
   - (B) engineer
   - (C) artist
   - (D) athlete

9. It was an **exhilarating** day. Everyone was amazed at the view from the top of the mountain.
   - (A) expressive
   - (B) exciting
   - (C) depressing
   - (D) additional

10. The deer faced the **adversity** of an especially cold winter. Deep snow covered the grass and shrubs.
    - (A) ascent
    - (B) hunter
    - (C) hardship
    - (D) interest

Review

1. I have been **confined** to my bedroom. I cannot come out until tonight.
   - (A) arrested
   - (B) limited
   - (C) expanded
   - (D) ordered

2. She liked the **acceptance** she felt in the club. The members made her feel welcome.
   - (A) application
   - (B) involvement
   - (C) association
   - (D) approval

Writing

Kitty O'Neil is a stuntwoman and race-car driver. Is there a career you might enjoy that involves adventure and daring? Tell about that career. What would you find exciting about this career?

Write a paragraph that identifies and discusses this adventurous career. Be sure to include details that describe the challenge this new career might present. Use some vocabulary words in your writing.

Turn to "My Personal Word List" on page 132. Write some words from the story or other words that you would like to know more about. Use a dictionary to find the meanings.

★ Read the story below. Think about the meanings of the **boldfaced** words. ★

Banner in the Sky

The Citadel was the greatest mountain in Switzerland, and Rudi Matt's father had lost his life trying to climb it. Now, standing on the highest point of the Citadel that had ever been reached, Rudi follows in his father's dream.

Rudi moved toward where the platform curved out of sight above the south face, and in a moment he was standing on the edge of an **abyss**. The platform still continued – or, rather, a narrow sloping ledge that formed an extension of the platform – and he carefully followed it around. He took four steps – five – six. And stopped. The ledge ended, petering out into the vertical walls of the Fortress. But from its farthest end he could see what he had hoped to see: the one break in the great cliff's defenses. No more than five yards beyond him, and starting at about the level at which he stood, a long cleft, or chimney, slanted upward through the otherwise unbroken rock.

This, he knew, was the way past the Fortress – the "key" to the upper mountain which his father had found fifteen years before. From where he stood he could not see the inside of the cleft, but its depth and angle were such that he was sure he could climb it. If – *if* – he could reach its base. . . .

Sliding to the very end of the ledge, he studied the gap beyond. There was no place to stand – he could see that at once; nor were there any cracks or knobs for handholds. But the wall, though vertical, was not altogether smooth. The rock between ledge and cleft protruded in a sort of wrinkled bulge, and if one could cling to the bulge for as much as a few seconds it would be possible to worm one's way across. Stepping out from the ledge, he inched out onto the bulge, using not only hands and feet, as in ordinary climbing, but all of his body that he could bring into play. He gripped the rock with arms and legs, pressed against it with chest and thighs, holding on not by any actual support but by the friction of his moving weight. Space wheeled beneath him. But once **committed**, he could not stop, or even hesitate, for such a maneuver had to be made quickly and in perfect rhythm, or it could not be made at all. Once he slipped – and once more – but both times the friction of his body held him, and a moment later, with a final twist and thrust, he swung off of the bulge into the base of the cleft.

His shirt and trousers were torn. His fingers were bleeding. But he scarcely noticed them. All he had eyes for was the long slanting shaft that now rose directly above him up the sheer wall of the Fortress. And yet, he thought suddenly with a great lift of the heart – he had been right; his father had been right. The cleft extended all the way to the top of the **precipice**. It was climbable. It was the way past the Fortress!

Instinctively he started up. . . . And in the next instant stopped. . . . For in that instant, for the first time since he had begun the ascent of the ridge, he thought of the hour. He glanced at the sun and saw that it was halfway between the **zenith** and the western horizon. There was no choice but soon to start down. But first he must have one glimpse, one moment's experience, of that high, hidden world above the Fortress.

The lower third of the cleft presented no difficulties. Then followed a stretch where it became a sort of narrow smooth-walled shaft, which at first glance appeared **impassable**; but, after some trial and error, he managed it by **bracing** his back against one wall, his feet against the other, and levering himself upward. Perhaps twenty minutes after entering the cleft, he emerged at its top onto a flat shelf above the cliff-face – the first human being to have passed the grim barrier of the Fortress.

Now, standing there in awe, Rudi Matt looked up at what no man's eyes had ever seen before. Starting directly in front of him, the southeast ridge, which had been blocked off by the Fortress, continued its upward progress, twisting on and on until it at last **merged** into the great bulge of the mountain's shoulder. So great was the distance that it seemed he was again back at the foot of the peak, rather than a third of the way up its flank. But distance in itself was unimportant, compared to the other thing he saw – and this was that the ridge appeared climbable to its very end. There would be obstacles. But no obstacles, so far as he could see, as **formidable** as the Fortress. Nothing that a skilled climber could not successfully **surmount**.

A deep, almost fierce joy welled in the boy's heart. Even though he must now turn back, he had already gone higher into the unknown than any man before him – including his father. He had proved that his father had been right: that there was a way past the Fortress, and that it was, indeed, the "key" to the mountain. With his own eyes he had seen the way ahead, leading upward and upward.

From Banner in the Sky, by
James Ramsey Ullman

★ Go back to the story. Underline any words or sentences that give you clues to the meanings of the **boldfaced** words. ★

CONTEXT CLUES

In each sentence, a word or phrase is underlined. Choose a word from the box to replace that word or phrase. Write the word on the line.

abyss	surmount	committed	zenith
merged	impassable	formidable	instinctively
bracing	precipice		

1. Climbing a mountain is a forbidding task. _____

2. A climber must be very dedicated to completing the task to try such a dangerous feat. _____

3. There are so many problems and hardships to overcome during a mountain climb. _____

4. Climbers are challenged by one very steep cliff after another.

   _____

5. There is the constant danger of falling into an extremely deep crack in the earth. _____

6. A trail may suddenly become not fit for traveling over because of falling rocks or snow and ice. _____

7. Blowing snow can play tricks with a climber's vision so that separate objects seem blended together. _____

8. Fortunately, a good climber learns to make decisions using knowledge he or she is born with. _____

9. For example, a climber may know just when giving support to his arms, legs, or back will prevent a fall. _____

10. And an experienced climber knows how to read the sky and to predict the number of hours from the time the sun reaches its point directly overhead to the hour when it sets. _____

CHALLENGE YOURSELF

Name two problems a student may need to surmount in school.

_____   _____

Name two things people do instinctively.

_____   _____

ANALOGIES

An **analogy** shows the relationship between pairs of words. Use the words in the box to complete the following analogies.

formidable	surmount	precipice
committed	merged	abyss

1. Controlled is to regulated as _____ is to dedicated.

2. Rigid is to flexible as _____ is to easy.

3. Peak is to height as _____ is to depth.

4. Wave is to ocean as _____ is to mountain.

5. Surrender is to yield as _____ is to overcome.

6. Bloomed is to wilted as _____ is to separated.

WORD DESCRIPTIONS

Read each word description. Then write the word from the box that best fits each description. Refer to the Dictionary, beginning on page 133, if you need help.

zenith	impassable	surmount
bracing	instinctively	

1. You might use this word to describe what purpose a column serves for a building. _____

2. This word describes what roads are like during a blizzard or a flood. _____

3. This word tells what determined people try to do when they meet an obstacle. _____

4. You can use this word to describe the place where the sun usually is at noon. _____

5. To explain how birds know when it is time to migrate south for the winter, you would use this word. _____

GET WISE TO TESTS

Directions: Read the sentence or sentences. Look for the best word to use in the blank. Mark the answer space for your choice.

If you are not sure which word completes the sentence, do the best you can. Try to choose the answer that makes the most sense.

1. When the kitten caught sight of the dog, she _____ hissed and arched her back.
   Ⓐ illegally   Ⓒ charmingly
   Ⓑ calmly   Ⓓ instinctively

2. Jay was the president of the club. He was _____ to attending all meetings.
   Ⓐ committed   Ⓒ voted
   Ⓑ merged   Ⓓ credited

3. The wrestler was huge. He looked like a _____ opponent.
   Ⓐ bracing   Ⓒ formidable
   Ⓑ helpless   Ⓓ merged

4. To enter the highway, the car _____ into the right lane.
   Ⓐ merged   Ⓒ encircled
   Ⓑ crashed   Ⓓ committed

5. He didn't fall because he was _____ himself against the wall.
   Ⓐ bracing   Ⓒ attracting
   Ⓑ painting   Ⓓ surmounting

6. The mountain goat could not get down. It was trapped on a steep _____.
   Ⓐ building   Ⓒ abyss
   Ⓑ boundary   Ⓓ precipice

7. The landslide blocked the cave entrance. It was _____ to us.
   Ⓐ open   Ⓒ impassable
   Ⓑ formidable   Ⓓ broken

8. The climber lost her pick. It fell into the icy _____.
   Ⓐ acre   Ⓒ precipice
   Ⓑ machinery   Ⓓ abyss

9. By taking swimming lessons, Jill hopes to _____ her fear of the water.
   Ⓐ surmount   Ⓒ digest
   Ⓑ continue   Ⓓ explain

10. We basked in the noonday warmth. The sun was at its _____.
    Ⓐ coolest   Ⓒ zenith
    Ⓑ side   Ⓓ precipice

Review

1. The police are trying to learn the _____ of this nameless child.
   Ⓐ occupation   Ⓒ disability
   Ⓑ address   Ⓓ identity

2. He is an _____ swimmer, the fastest and the best on the team.
   Ⓐ active   Ⓒ ace
   Ⓑ endless   Ⓓ anxious

3. My mother injured her back and cannot walk. That _____ will keep her out of work for several months.
   Ⓐ wheelchair   Ⓒ disease
   Ⓑ disability   Ⓓ retirement

4. Riding in a very fast boat is an _____ experience. It's so exciting to zip over the waves.
   Ⓐ interesting Ⓒ explosive
   Ⓑ annual   Ⓓ exhilarating

Writing

Think about the risks Rudi took as he tried to conquer the Citadel. In your opinion, was he wise or foolish in trying to pursue his father's dream?

Write a paragraph giving your opinion of Rudi's actions and goal. Be sure to give several reasons that back up your opinion. Use some vocabulary words in your writing.

_____

_____

_____

_____

_____

_____

_____

_____

_____

_____

_____

_____

_____

_____

_____

_____

_____

Turn to "My Personal Word List" on page 132. Write some words from the story or other words that you would like to know more about. Use a dictionary to find the meanings.

★ Read the story below. Think about the meanings of the **boldfaced** words. ★

West Through the Night

Rain was falling and the sky was pitch black. Two thousand feet above the Atlantic Ocean, in a tiny single-engine plane, Beryl Markham was flying — alone. She was attempting to become the first person ever to fly from England to America across the rugged North Atlantic. In 1936 not many pilots, even the most **competent** and able, would try such a feat. But Markham had made a **commitment**, and she was determined to fulfill her promise.

Suddenly, the plane's motor stalled. Markham was far from land, without the hope of rescue. She watched the gauge that measured the plane's height spin wildly downward. At 300 feet above the crashing waves, she thought it was the end. There was no **indication**, no sign, that the plane would recover. Then, just as suddenly, the motor kicked back to life!

That was not the last exciting moment in this historic flight. After flying west through the night, Markham reached the coast of Newfoundland in the early morning. Soon after she sighted land, the plane's single motor shuddered and died. Markham tried everything she knew to restart it, but her **extensive** efforts all met with failure. She unhappily **conceded**, admitting defeat, and turned her attention instead to landing safely. Below her were boulders that could tear the plane apart. But by turning and gliding and using every **maneuver** she had ever learned, the pilot landed in thick, deep mud.

It was an **emotional** moment for Markham. She felt both great joy and disappointment. After all, hadn't she flown for 21 hours and 25 minutes and crossed the North Atlantic? This was a new world record. Yet Markham had not attained her targeted destination — New York.

Still, as news of her success spread, people were impressed by her achievement. Her courage and **fortitude** in attempting such a risky flight had earned their **esteem**. What these people did not know was that Markham had faced many dangers throughout her life in British East Africa. As a pilot, first carrying mail, then tracking elephants, she had risked crash landings in remote areas. To Markham, hard work and effort were necessary to meet each challenge and to get the job done. **Diligence** and courage were the qualities that helped her set a world record.

★ Go back to the story. Underline the words or sentences that give you a clue to the meaning of each **boldfaced** word. ★

CONTEXT CLUES

Read each pair of sentences. Look for clues to help you complete one of the sentences with a word from the box. Write the word on the line.

commitment	indication	extensive	conceded
competent	fortitude	esteem	diligence
maneuver	emotional		

1. When Beryl was four years old, her mother returned to England, leaving her child behind in Africa. Beryl managed to overcome

   this _____ hardship by becoming independent.

2. She explored the countryside with her father and her friends. In

   this way, she built up an _____ knowledge of East Africa.

3. Beryl's father trained champion horses. For years, Beryl worked

   with _____ until she mastered this same skill.

4. When Beryl was seventeen, her father _____ that he was bored with East Africa. He admitted to her that he was planning to move to Peru.

5. Beryl would be left to handle the horse ranch alone. Her father felt

   that she was quite _____ to do this job.

6. By this time, Beryl's love for and _____ to Africa were very deep. She willingly agreed to stay there.

7. Beryl had also developed an interest in flying. She took lessons,

   learned quickly, and gave every _____ of becoming a fine pilot.

8. In those days, pilots had few instruments to help them control their

   planes. Beryl learned the difficult _____ of landing a plane on rough ground at night anyway.

9. She flew several rescue missions alone, and over great distances. In this way, she became well known in her own country and won

   the _____ of other pilots.

10. She had a sense of adventure, much experience, and the courage to

    tackle tough assignments. It was this _____ that led her to risk the long voyage over the Atlantic Ocean.

WORD ORIGINS

Knowing the origin of a word can help you understand its meaning. Read each word origin. Then write each word from the box next to its origin.

emotional	diligence	esteem
commitment	conceded	maneuver

1. from Latin <u>diligentia</u>, carefulness _____

2. from Latin <u>aestimare</u>, to value _____

3. from Latin <u>concedere</u>, to yield _____

4. from French <u>manoeuvre</u>, action, scheme _____

5. from Latin <u>committere</u>, to connect _____

6. from Latin <u>emovere</u>, to stir up _____

REWRITING SENTENCES

Rewrite each sentence using one of the vocabulary words from the box.

maneuver	competent	fortitude
indication	esteem	extensive

1. That skillful move may win him the chess championship.

_____

2. She has the courage to reach her goal.

_____

3. The mayor presented far-reaching plans to help the homeless.

_____

4. We hold our teacher in high regard.

_____

5. A child is not qualified to drive a school bus.

_____

6. There is no sign that the blizzard will hit this area.

_____

GET WISE TO TESTS

Directions: Read each sentence. Pick the word that best completes the sentence. Mark the answer space for that word.

Before you choose an answer, try reading the sentence with each answer choice. This will help you choose an answer that makes sense.

1. The gray clouds are an _____ of rain.
   A ○ absolute
   B ○ indication
   C ○ stormy
   D ○ esteem

2. He has crashed twice so he is not _____ to fly a plane.
   A ○ pilot
   B ○ conceded
   C ○ study
   D ○ competent

3. The weary candidate _____ the election.
   A ○ vote
   B ○ maneuver
   C ○ win
   D ○ conceded

4. I can't make a _____ to that job right now.
   A ○ hire
   B ○ indication
   C ○ committed
   D ○ commitment

5. That romantic movie appeals to the _____ side of me.
   A ○ viewed
   B ○ emotional
   C ○ competent
   D ○ injustice

6. Their _____ brought them through safely.
   A ○ fortitude
   B ○ bravely
   C ○ obedient
   D ○ extensive

7. He led an _____ discussion about the novel.
   A ○ observe
   B ○ experiment
   C ○ extensive
   D ○ indication

8. You have earned my _____.
   A ○ conceded
   B ○ like
   C ○ devotions
   D ○ esteem

9. It will take much _____ to finish this task.
   A ○ diligence
   B ○ machines
   C ○ competent
   D ○ determine

10. That _____ is too difficult to attempt.
    A ○ maneuver
    B ○ numerous
    C ○ seventy
    D ○ competent

Review

1. We must find a way to _____ this problem.
   A ○ purchase
   B ○ surmount
   C ○ zenith
   D ○ solving

2. The noonday sun is at its _____ in the sky.
   A ○ peaked
   B ○ lowest
   C ○ impassable
   D ○ zenith

3. A mouse knows _____ to run from a cat.
   A ○ instinctively
   B ○ learns
   C ○ nothing
   D ○ today

4. I am _____ to the idea that students have their own government.
   A ○ bracing
   B ○ impassable
   C ○ committed
   D ○ persuade

5. After the wind storm, the roads were _____ because of fallen branches.
   A ○ mess
   B ○ impassable
   C ○ speed
   D ○ wooden

Writing

Think about the characteristics of heroes like Beryl Markham. Among them are courage, diligence, pride, and a sense of adventure. Many people have the same characteristics, but they do not become famous as Markham did. They might be called heroes without fame. Such a person might be someone you know or someone you've read about.

Write a paragraph about one of these unknown heroes. Tell what makes this person heroic and worthy of admiration. Use some vocabulary words in your writing.

_____

_____

_____

_____

_____

_____

_____

_____

_____

_____

_____

_____

_____

_____

_____

_____

_____

_____

_____

Turn to "My Personal Word List" on page 132. Write some words from the story or other words that you would like to know more about. Use a dictionary to find the meanings.

★ Read the story below. Think about the meanings of the **boldfaced** words. ★

Underwater Explorer

Jacques Cousteau put on his new diving goggles and waded into the sea. The twenty-six-year-old Frenchman had enjoyed swimming ever since he was a boy. Now, as he dropped under the surface of the water, an entirely new world opened up. An **array** of fish, seaweed, and rocks appeared around him. Yet despite this colorful variety of sea life, he felt a sense of peace in this ocean world. At that moment, Jacques Cousteau decided to become a deep-sea explorer.

The year was 1936, and little was known about ocean diving. Diving equipment was dangerous, heavy, and bulky. Cousteau began working to make diving safer and easier. He started wearing rubber fins so he could swim faster underwater. Later he invented a breathing system that used tanks to carry oxygen. This system allowed divers to **inhale** and **exhale**, or breathe in and out, underwater.

Ten years later, Cousteau set up the Undersea Research Group with other divers who were exploring the deep sea. He and his **colleagues** explored shipwrecks. They also studied marine life.

In 1950, Cousteau realized one of his greatest ambitions. With the help of a wealthy friend, he bought a research ship, the *Calypso*. While exploring the oceans, divers on the *Calypso* often **confronted** sharks and other dangers. The **fearlessness** of the explorers became well known. Cousteau has written several books about their experiences. He has also produced many films about sea life. Three of the films have won Academy Awards.

As Cousteau grows older, he spends more time fighting **environmental** problems. During his long diving career, he saw that pollution was killing ocean life by destroying the homes of many fish. In the 1960s and 1970s, his television series *The Undersea World of Jacques Cousteau* dramatized underwater exploration and concern for the health of the ocean. From his own experiences, Cousteau knew that **cooperation** is the key to success. People must work together to protect sea life.

Jacques Cousteau's accomplishments have made him one of the **dominant** figures in the field of ocean study. This powerful position also makes him an important **adviser** to a new generation of sea explorers. Today, on a new *Calypso*, he is sailing boldly ahead on a mission to preserve our world.

★ Go back to the story. Underline the words or sentences that give you a clue to the meaning of each **boldfaced** word. ★

USING CONTEXT

Meanings for the vocabulary words are given below. Go back to the story and read each sentence that contains a vocabulary word. If you still cannot tell the meaning, look for clues in the sentences that come before and after the one with the vocabulary word. Write each word in front of its meaning.

array	confronted	environmental	inhale
adviser	colleagues	fearlessness	exhale
dominant	cooperation		

1. _____ : fellow members of a profession; co-workers

2. _____ : large assortment or collection

3. _____ : to breathe in air through the nose or mouth

4. _____ : the state of being very brave; unafraid

5. _____ : a person who offers advice or information on a particular subject

6. _____ : the act or process of working together with others to achieve a common goal

7. _____ : to breathe out air through the nose or mouth

8. _____ : most influential; central

9. _____ : having to do with the surroundings, with nature

10. _____ : came face to face with; faced boldly

CHALLENGE YOURSELF

Name two activities at school that require an <u>adviser</u>.

_____   _____

Name two activities that require <u>cooperation</u>.

_____   _____

Name two <u>environmental</u> problems in the United States today.

_____   _____

CLOZE PARAGRAPH

Use the words in the box to complete the passage. Then reread the passage to be sure it makes sense.

array	confronted	colleagues	inhale
exhale	cooperation	fearlessness	dominant
adviser	environmental		

My uncle and his friends started a diving club. Besides diving together, most of the members are also business

(1) _____. The club members began by trying to learn as much as possible about diving. They hired a professional diver to give them instructions. This teacher would also be the club's

(2) _____ when the group began to plan diving trips.

The instruction started with learning how to use fins, tanks, and weights. The student divers spent long hours in a swimming pool practicing with their scuba equipment. They learned the proper

way to (3) _____, or breathe in, and to

(4) _____, or breathe out. They learned special

methods of (5) _____ that could be used if one diver needed emergency help underwater.

After the club members learned the basic skills of diving, they went

on their first deep-sea diving trip. They (6) _____ problems that they had not faced during their training. They met these challenges without hesitating, and their teacher congratulated them for

their (7) _____ in the face of danger. They did well because they were prepared and understood what to do in an emergency.

The divers were always delighted when they saw a great variety of

sea life. On almost every trip, they saw a vast (8) _____ of ocean plants and animals. In many cases, though, pollution was affecting the sea. The divers were so upset by this

(9) _____ problem that they decided to devote some time to helping to solve it.

Club members invited a speaker from the Cousteau Society to tell them how they could help. They wrote to government officials to express their concern about the welfare of the oceans. Diving had been

their (10) _____ interest at first. Now, like Jacques Cousteau, they were interested in everything that had to do with the world of the sea.

WORD GAME

The underlined letters in each sentence below are part of one of the vocabulary words. Use the underlined letters and the context of the sentence to determine the correct vocabulary word. Write the word on the line.

array	confronted	environmental	colleagues
exhale	dominant	fearlessness	inhale
adviser	cooperation		

1. After the company dug the <u>iron</u> out of the mountain, they realized that they had destroyed the homes of many animals.

   _____

2. He took a deep breath and noticed how sweet it smelled <u>in</u> the

   flowering orange grove.   _____

3. Jack, his two sisters, and his father worked together for a whole week to build a new chicken <u>coop</u> that the fox couldn't get into.

   _____

4. The soldiers were given <u>less</u> time than normal to get ready for the big battle, but they still marched bravely to the fight.

   _____

5. My friend, <u>Ray</u>, and I like to walk together in the meadow, which is filled with hundreds of colorful flowers and fascinating

   insects.   _____

6. The <u>ad</u> said they were looking for a person who could counsel

   students who needed guidance.   _____

7. I <u>do</u> think it is important that the club leader be the person who has

   the most power and influence.   _____

8. The bus driver demanded that the angry riders come to the <u>front</u> of the bus and tell him face-to-face what they were upset about.

   _____

9. Most of the people who work in my mother's office are also

   members of her bowling <u>league</u>.   _____

10. <u>Hal</u> has such a terrible cold, his chest rattles every time

    he breathes out.   _____

Directions: Read each sentence carefully. Then choose the best answer to complete each sentence. Mark the space for the answer you have chosen.

This test will show you how well you understand the meaning of the words. Think about the meaning of the boldfaced word before you choose your answer.

1. An **array** of goods means that there are _____ to choose from.
   - (A) many
   - (B) four
   - (C) none
   - (D) few

2. A person who displays **fearlessness** is _____.
   - (A) crazy
   - (B) frightened
   - (C) brave
   - (D) foolish

3. When someone has **confronted** a dangerous situation, he has _____ it.
   - (A) eaten
   - (B) faced
   - (C) retrieved
   - (D) pointed

4. When you work in **cooperation** with someone, you work _____ her.
   - (A) against
   - (B) without
   - (C) after
   - (D) with

5. When you **inhale**, you breathe _____.
   - (A) out
   - (B) heavy
   - (C) under
   - (D) in

6. **Environmental** experts study the _____.
   - (A) surroundings
   - (B) clothes
   - (C) space
   - (D) moon

7. A **dominant** color will be the one you _____ most in a room.
   - (A) scratch
   - (B) donate
   - (C) tempt
   - (D) notice

8. When you **exhale**, you _____ your breath.
   - (A) release
   - (B) accept
   - (C) outline
   - (D) excuse

9. A teacher's **colleagues** are other _____.
   - (A) students
   - (B) teachers
   - (C) schools
   - (D) parents

10. A clothing **adviser** would _____ clothes for you to wear.
   - (A) sew
   - (B) steal
   - (C) fold
   - (D) recommend

Review

1. An **emotional** moment is one filled with strong _____.
   - (A) feelings
   - (B) odors
   - (C) muscles
   - (D) lights

2. A **competent** worker is one who is _____ to do a job.
   - (A) unwilling
   - (B) happy
   - (C) qualified
   - (D) sorry

3. An **extensive** collection of coins is one that contains _____ coins.
   - (A) old
   - (B) new
   - (C) fountain
   - (D) many

4. A worker who shows **diligence** is _____.
   - (A) lazy
   - (B) ill-mannered
   - (C) careless
   - (D) hard-working

Environmental issues have concerned Jacques Cousteau and others. What are some of the ways that people are harming the earth?

   Write an editorial for a magazine that tells about one practice that is harming our environment. In your editorial, describe the practice. Explain why you believe the practice is or is not justified. Use some vocabulary words in your writing.

Turn to "My Personal Word List" on page 132. Write some words from the story or other words that you would like to know more about. Use a dictionary to find the meanings.

★ To review the words in Lessons 17–20, turn to page 129. ★

REVIEW

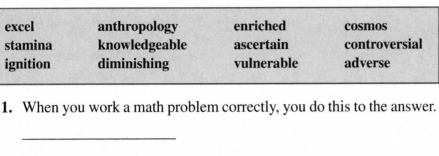

Read each clue. Then write the word from the box that fits the clue. Use the Dictionary if you need help.

excel	anthropology	enriched	cosmos
stamina	knowledgeable	ascertain	controversial
ignition	diminishing	vulnerable	adverse

1. When you work a math problem correctly, you do this to the answer.
   _____

2. If you swim in waters full of sharks, you make yourself this.
   _____

3. If you want to learn about human cultures and ways of life, this is what you should study. _____

4. If you learn to play chess and then become a champion player, you do this. _____

5. When roads become icy, the driving conditions can be described with this word. _____

6. When people have made great contributions to a field of study, we say they have done this to it. _____

7. Someone who is an expert in a field of study could be described with this word. _____

8. If you travel throughout the whole universe, you explore this.
   _____

9. When this occurs, a rocket ship lifts off. _____

10. If you are spending more and more and have less and less money, your savings are doing this. _____

11. If many people argue about a subject, the subject can be described with this word. _____

12. Running a marathon requires this. _____

Read each question. Think about the meaning of the underlined word. Then use yes or no to answer the question. Use the Dictionary if you need help.

1. Would it be necessary to excavate in order to build a tunnel? _____

2. Would you expect to find urbanites living on a dairy farm? _____

3. If you have been authorized to run your school, do you have permission to take charge of it? _____

4. Would most people have feelings of melancholy if they heard a cheerful song? _____

5. Do you see your classmates with frequency? _____

6. If you are eligible to vote in an election, are you allowed to vote? _____

7. When a game is informal, does it have a lot of rules? _____

8. On a clear night in the country, might you see a profusion of stars? _____

9. Is it accurate to say that a song of praise written in someone's honor dignifies that person? _____

10. Would most students enjoy a timeless homework assignment? _____

11. If you want to convey a message with your voice, should you be silent? _____

12. If you are not interested in sports, are your feelings about sports ardent? _____

13. Could a picnic in the country be described as pastoral? _____

14. To learn about birds, should you study architecture? _____

15. Could the food, language, and dress of a group of people be called their cultural features? _____

Read each clue. Then write the word from the box that fits the clue. Use the Dictionary if you need help.

inadequate	winch	hemisphere	audible
disastrous	mingled	anticipate	seismic
fauna	altered	disrupts	halfheartedly

1. When you work without interest or enthusiasm, you do it this way.

   _____

2. This is another word for the deer, rabbits, and other animals in a forest. _____

3. Someone who interrupts a conversation does this.

   _____

4. If you look forward to your birthday party, you do this.

   _____

5. This word refers to one half of the globe. _____

6. When you speak loudly enough to be heard, your voice is this.

   _____

7. If you are trapped in a blizzard and have no coat or sweater, your clothing could be called this. _____

8. If you got your hair cut, you did this to your appearance.

   _____

9. Earthquakes, tornadoes, and tidal waves can often be this.

   _____

10. The waves that result from an earthquake are called this.

    _____

11. When you use a machine to lift a large object, you do this.

    _____

12. When things are mixed together, we sometimes use this word to describe them. _____

REVIEW

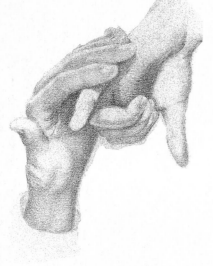

Read each question. Think about the meaning of the underlined word. Then use <u>yes</u> or <u>no</u> to answer the question. Use the Dictionary if you need help.

1. Can a dog and cat be <u>identical</u>? _____
2. If your choices of ice cream flavors are <u>confined</u> to chocolate and vanilla, can you have strawberry? _____
3. Are <u>dialects</u> parts of a telephone? _____
4. If you have a <u>passionate</u> interest in skating, would you probably want to see Olympic skaters compete? _____
5. Is confidence something that is <u>tangible</u>? _____
6. Does an actor obtain <u>exposure</u> from starring in many movies and television programs? _____
7. When writing has <u>clarity</u>, is it hard to understand? _____
8. If drivers <u>exceeded</u> the speed limit, did they drive below it? _____
9. If you want silence, should you <u>evoke</u> sounds? _____
10. Is an <u>eventful</u> day likely to be one you will remember well? _____
11. If you were <u>amazingly</u> tired, did you have a lot of energy? _____
12. Is it possible to <u>transmit</u> a message? _____
13. If you want a friend to learn something, would it help to <u>instill</u> the information? _____
14. Could a person eat a <u>tussle</u>? _____
15. If you want to know the <u>figurative</u> meaning of a phrase, should you rely on the dictionary meaning of each word? _____

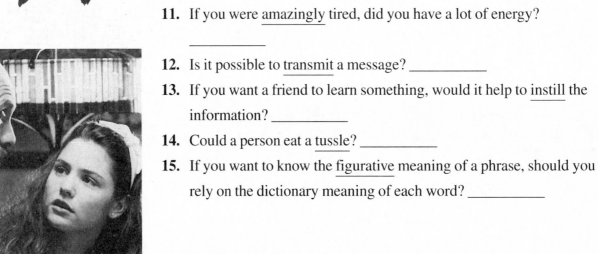

Read each clue. Then write the word from the box that fits the clue. Use the Dictionary if you need help.

confronted	emotional	antics	exhilarating
instinctively	coordination	exhale	zenith
array	commitment	esteem	merged

1. If you want to be a good dancer, this comes in handy.

   _____

2. A thrilling ride at a carnival could also be called this.

   _____

3. If you stand at the top of a mountain, you are at this point.

   _____

4. If you think highly of someone, you have this for that person.

   _____

5. If two armies went to battle, they did this to each other.

   _____

6. This is what two roads did at the point where they met.

   _____

7. We use this word to describe things that have to do with feelings.

   _____

8. When we breathe, we do this after we inhale.

   _____

9. When the team made a promise to win, they made this.

   _____

10. We use this word to describe some things that we do without thinking. _____

11. If you are a stuntperson, you do these. _____

12. A number of items to choose from could be called this.

   _____

REVIEW AND WRITE

Many of the stories in *Vocabulary Connections* deal with courage. In some stories, it is physical courage – the willingness to attempt a difficult race, climb a mountain, or fly across the ocean. In other stories, it is moral courage – the courage necessary to risk failure, embarrassment, or unpopularity.

Go back through the book and select an example of each type of courage. Explain how physical courage or moral courage was shown in each example. Tell what people can learn from each example. Use some vocabulary words you have learned.

MY PERSONAL WORD LIST

This is your word list. Here you can write words from the stories. You can also write other words that you would like to know more about. Use a dictionary to find the meaning of each word. Then write the meaning next to the word.

UNIT 1

_____
_____
_____
_____
_____
_____
_____

UNIT 2

_____
_____
_____
_____
_____
_____
_____

MY PERSONAL WORD LIST

UNIT 3
THE EARTH IS MOVING! ——————————————————————

——————————————————————

——————————————————————

——————————————————————

——————————————————————

——————————————————————

——————————————————————

UNIT 4
SENDING MESSAGES ——————————————————————

——————————————————————

——————————————————————

——————————————————————

——————————————————————

——————————————————————

——————————————————————

UNIT 5
SPIRIT OF ADVENTURE ——————————————————————

——————————————————————

——————————————————————

——————————————————————

——————————————————————

——————————————————————

——————————————————————

DICTIONARY

ENTRY

Each word in a dictionary is called an **entry word**. Study the parts of an entry in the sample shown below. Think about how each part will help you when you read and write.

(1) **Entry Word** An entry word is boldfaced. A dot is used to divide the word into syllables.

(2) **Pronunciation** This special spelling shows you how to say the word. Look at the pronunciation key below. It tells you the symbols that stand for sounds.

(3) **Part of Speech** The abbreviation tells you the part of speech. In this entry *v.* stands for verb.

(4) **Words with Spelling Changes** When the spelling of a word changes after *-ed* and *-ing* are added, it is shown in an entry.

(5) **Definition** A definition is given for each entry word. The definition tells what the word means.

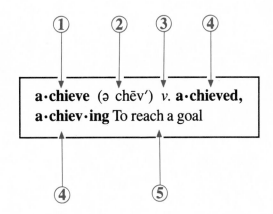

① ② ③ ④

a·chieve (ə chēv′) *v.* **a·chieved, a·chiev·ing** To reach a goal

④ ⑤

PRONUNCIATION KEY

A **pronunciation key** is a helpful tool. It shows you the symbols, or special signs, for the sounds in English. Next to each symbol is a sample word for that sound. Use the key to help you with the pronunciation given after each entry word.

a	at, bad	d	dear, soda, bad
ā	ape, pain, day, break	f	five, defend, leaf, off, cough, elephant
ä	father, car, heart	g	game, ago, fog, egg
âr	care, pair, bear, their, where	h	hat, ahead
e	end, pet, said, heaven, friend	hw	white, whether, which
ē	equal, me, feet, team, piece, key	j	joke, enjoy, gem, page, edge
i	it, big, English, hymn	k	kite, bakery, seek, tack, cat
ī	ice, fine, lie, my	l	lid, sailor, feel, ball, allow
îr	ear, deer, here, pierce	m	man, family, dream
o	odd, hot, watch	n	not, final, pan, knife
ō	old, oat, toe, low	ng	long, singer, pink
ô	coffee, all, taught, law, fought	p	pail, repair, soap, happy
ôr	order, fork, horse, story, pour	r	ride, parent, wear, more, marry
oi	oil, toy	s	sit, aside, pets, cent, pass
ou	out, now	sh	shoe, washer, fish, mission, nation
u	up, mud, love, double	t	tag, pretend, fat, button, dressed
ū	use, mule, cue, feud, few	th	thin, panther, both
ü	rule, true, food	<u>th</u>	this, mother, smooth
u̇	put, wood, should	v	very, favor, wave
ûr	burn, hurry, term, bird, word, courage	w	wet, weather, reward
ə	about, taken, pencil, lemon, circus	y	yes, onion
b	bat, above, job	z	zoo, lazy, jazz, rose, dogs, houses
ch	chin, such, match	zh	vision, treasure, seizure

Dictionary

A

a•byss (ə bis´) *n.* A very deep space. page 108

ac•cept•ance (ak sep´təns) *n.* The state of being approved of. page 95

ac•claim (ə klām´) *n.* Recognition; approval. page 23

ac•cu•ra•cy (ak´yər ə sē) *n.* The state of being correct and exact. page 71

ace (ās) *n.* A person who is an expert in a certain field; the best. That athlete is an ace at golf. page 102

ac•ro•bat•ics (ak´rə bat´iks) *n.* Stunts that require strength and good balance. page 102

a•cute (ə kūt´) *adj.* Extreme. Swimmers may suffer from acute sunburn if they fail to protect their skin. page 23

ad•join•ing (ə joi´ning) *adj.* Next to; nearby. page 66

ad•verse (ad vûrs´, ad´vûrs) *adj.* Difficult; unfavorable. page 23

ad•ver•si•ty (ad vûr´si tē) *n.* **ad•ver•si•ties** Trouble; difficulty. page 102

ad•vis•er (ad vī´zər) *n.* A person who gives advice. page 119

ag•gres•sive (ə gres´iv) *adj.* Bold; forceful. page 23

ag•ile (aj´əl, aj´īl) *adj.* Able to move quickly and easily; nimble. page 104

a•gil•i•ty (ə jil´ i tē) *n.* The ability to move quickly and easily. A professional dancer needs agility to dance well. page 102

ag•o•niz•ing (ag´ə nīz´ing) *adj.* Causing great pain. page 23

al•ter (ôl´tər) *v.* To change. page 66

al•ter•nate (ôl´tər nāt´) *v.* **al•ter•nat•ed, al•ter•nat•ing** To happen by turns; go back and forth. page 68

a•maz•ing•ly (ə māz´ing lē) *adv.* In an astonishing or surprising way. page 90

an•a•lyze (an´ə līz´) *v.* **an•a•lyzed, an•a•ly•zing** To study carefully; to find out what something is made of. page 18

an•thro•pol•o•gy (an´thrə pol´ə jē) *n.* The science that studies human cultures and ways of life. page 6

an•tic (an´tik) *n.* A stunt; trick. page 102

an•tic•i•pate (an tis´ə pāt´) *v.* **an•tic•i•pat•ed, an•tic•i•pat•ing** To know beforehand; expect. page 71

ap•ti•tude (ap´ti tüd´, ap´ti tūd´) *n.* Natural ability. page 23

ar•chae•ol•o•gist (är´kē ol´ə jist) *n.* A scientist who studies relics from the ancient past. page 42

ar•chi•tec•ture (är´ki tek´chər) *n.* The science and art of planning and designing buildings and other structures. page 47

ar•dent (är´dənt) *adj.* Having or showing great enthusiasm. page 30

ar•ray (ə rā´) *n.* Variety; large collection. page 119

as•cent (ə sent´) *n.* Rise; upward movement. The ascent of the rocket was swift. page 13

as•cer•tain (as´ər tān´) *v.* To find out; discover for certain. Space scientists are eager to ascertain the climate of Mars. page 18

as•sur•ance (ə shùr´əns) *n.* Confidence; freedom from doubt. page 102

as•sure (e shùr´) *v.* **as•sured, as•sur•ing** To make certain; say with confidence. page 104

au•di•ble (ô´də bəl) *adj.* Able to be heard. page 54

au•then•tic (ô then´tik) *adj.* Real; in agreement with fact. page 6

au•thor•i•za•tion (ô´thər ə zā´shən) *n.* The giving of power or command. page 49

au•thor•ize (ô´thə rīz´) *v.* **au•thor•ized, au•thor•iz•ing** To give power to; give the right to decide. page 47

a•vert (ə vûrt´) *v.* To prevent; avoid. page 71

B

be•wil•der•ing (bi wil´dər ing) *adj.* Causing confusion. page 78

bi•o•graph•i•cal (bī´ə graf´i kəl) *adj.* Having to do with the facts and events in a person's life. page 30

bit•ter•ness (bit´ər nis) *n.* Feelings of resentment and ill will. page 84

blight•ed (blīt´id) *adj.* Damaged; ruined. The blighted roses turned dark brown. page 66

bo•nan•za (bə nan´zə) *n.* Something that brings wealth or happiness. page 42

brace (brās) *v.* **braced, brac•ing** To hold something in place. page 109

C

cer•e•mo•ni•al (ser´ə mō´nē əl) *adj.* Having to do with a special occasion. Native Americans sometimes perform ceremonial dances to celebrate the harvest. page 6

char•ac•ter (kar´ik tər) *n.* A symbol that stands for an object, idea, or sound. The Chinese have a character for the sun that looks like a sun. page 78

char•ac•ter•is•tic (kar´ik tə ris´tik) *adj.* Typical; making a person, group, or thing different or distinct. page 42

clar•i•ty (klar´i tē) *n.* **clar•i•ties** Sharpness of focus; clearness. page 90

close•ness (klōs´nis´) *n.* Nearness in space or in feeling. page 90

col•league (kol´ēg) *n.* A fellow worker. page 119

com•mit•ment (kə mit´mənt) *n.* A promise; something one pledges to do. page 114

com•mit•ted (kə mit´id) *adj.* Dedicated to a course of action. page 108

com•pe•tent (kom´pi tənt) *adj.* Capable; qualified. The hiker is also a competent mountain climber. page 114

com•ple•tion (kəm plē´shən) *n.* The act of finishing; conclusion. page 47

com•pute (kəm pūt´) *v.* **com•put•ed, com•put•ing** To figure out by using mathematics. page 71

con•cede (kən sēd´) *v.* **con•ced•ed, con•ced•ing** To admit or give up. The politician conceded the election to his opponent. page 114

con•fine (kən fīn´) *v.* **con•fined, con•fin•ing** To limit; hold in one place. page 95

con•front (kən frunt´) *v.* To face. page 119

con•science (kon´shəns) *n.* The ability to tell right from wrong. page 30

con•tem•po•rar•y (kən tem´pə rer´ē) *adj.* Belonging to the present time; current. page 6

con•ti•nu•i•ty (kon´tə nü´i tē, kon´tə nū´i tē) *n.* **con•ti•nu•i•ties** The state of being uninterrupted; a connection that remains unbroken over time. Customs in a family give it continuity. page 42

con•tour (kon´tür) *n.* The outline; edge. This map shows the contour of the island. page 54

con•trap•tion (kən trap´shən) *n.* A device or machine. page 90

con•trib•u•tor (kən trib´yə tər) *n.* A person who gives knowledge, time, or money. page 71

con•tro•ver•sial (kon´trə vûr´shəl) *adj.* Causing questions and arguments. page 18

con•ven•tion•al (kən ven´shə nəl) *adj.* Traditional; ordinary and usual. page 95

con•vey (kən vā´) *v.* To show; express. page 30

co•op•er•a•tion (kō op´ə rā´shən) *n.* The act or state of working together. page 119

co•or•di•na•tion (kō ôr´də nā´shən) *n.* Smooth and skillful body movements. page 102

cope (kōp) *v.* **coped, cop•ing** To deal successfully with difficulties. page 66

cor•re•spon•dence (kôr´ə spon´dəns, kor´ə spon´dəns) *n.* Written messages. page 90

cos•mos (koz´məs, koz´mōs) *n.* All of space; the universe. page 18

course (kôrs) *v.* **coursed, cours•ing** To move quickly. page 61

cre•a•tion (krē ā´shən) *n.* The act of making something new. page 49

cre•a•tiv•i•ty (krē´ā tiv´i tē) *n.* The ability to create; the quality of having many original ideas. page 47

cru•cial (krü´shəl) *adj.* Critically important. page 54

cul•tur•al (kul´chər əl) *adj.* Having to do with all the beliefs and activities of a particular group of people. page 42

D

de•rive (di rīv´) *v.* **de•rived, de•riv•ing** To come from a source or origin. page 6

de•scrip•tive (di skrip´tiv) *adj.* Giving a picture of; showing. page 42

de•struc•tive (di struk´tiv) *adj.* Causing great damage. page 54

dev•as•tate (dev´ə stāt´) *v.* **dev•as•tat•ed, dev•as•tat•ing** To ruin; destroy. page 71

di•a•lect (dī´ə lekt´) *n.* A form of speech spoken in a certain area. page 78

dig•ni•fy (dig´nə fī´) *v.* **dig•ni•fied, dig•ni•fy•ing** To show respect toward; honor. page 47

dig•ni•ty (dig´ni tē) *n.* **dig•ni•ties** The state of being respected and honored. page 49

dil•i•gence (dil´i jəns) *n.* Hard, continuous effort. page 114

dil•i•gent (dil´i jənt) *adj.* Done with great care and effort. page 6

di•mi•nish•ing (di min´ish ing) *verb.* Growing smaller. page 13

dis•a•bil•i•ty (dis´ə bil´i tē) *n.* **dis•a•bil•i•ties** A lack of ability to do a certain thing. page 102

dis•a•ble (dis ā´bəl) *v.* **dis•a•bled, dis•a•bling** To make unable; destroy a physical or mental ability. page 104

dis•ad•van•tage (dis´ad van´tij) *n.* An unfavorable circumstance or condition. page 95

dis•as•ter (di zas´tər) *n.* A terrible event; catastrophe. page 68

dis•as•trous (di zas´trəs) *adj.* Terrible; causing people to suffer. page 66

dis•heart•en (dis här´tən) *v.* To discourage; make one lose heart. page 23

dis•rupt (dis rupt´) *v.* To break or interrupt. page 54

dom•i•nant (dom´ə nənt) *adj.* Most powerful; ruling. A principal is a dominant person in a school. page 119

dor•mant (dôr´mənt) *adj.* In a state of inactivity; not operating. page 61

E

el•i•gi•ble (el´i jə bəl) *adj.* Allowed; qualified. page 47

e•mo•tion•al (i mō´shə nəl) *adj.* Marked by strong feelings. page 114

em•pha•size (em´fə sīz´) *v.* **em•pha•sized, em•pha•siz•ing** To give special importance to. page 30

en•grav•ing (en grā´ving) *n.* A picture that is cut into a hard surface. page 42

en•light•en (en lī´tən) *v.* To help to understand; give information. page 30

en•rich (en rich´) *v.* To make richer; add to. page 6

en•vi•ron•men•tal (en vī´rən men´təl) *adj.* Having to do with the surrounding in which things live. page 119

es•teem (e stēm´) *n.* Respect; high opinion. page 114

eth•nic (eth´nik) *adj.* Having to do with religious, racial, national, or cultural groups. page 96

e•val•u•ate (i val´ū āt´) *v.* **e•val•u•at•ed, e•val•u•at•ing** To measure or judge. page 71

e•vent•ful (i vent´fəl) *adj.* Filled with important happenings. page 84

e•voke (i vōk´) *v.* **e•voked, e•vok•ing** To call forth. The old movies evoked many memories. page 95

ex•ca•vate (eks´kə vāt´) *v.* **ex•cav•at•ed, ex•cav•at•ing** To dig up. page 42

ex•ceed (ek sēd´) *v.* To go beyond. The driver exceeded the speed limit. page 90

ex•cel (ek sel´) *v.* **ex•celled, ex•cel•ling** To outdo; do very well. page 23

ex•clud•ing (ek sklüd´ing) *adj.* Leaving out. page 78

ex•ert (eg zûrt´) *v.* To put into action; use. page 54

ex•hale (eks hāl´) *v.* **exhaled, exhaling** To breathe out. page 119

ex•hil•a•rat•ing (eg zil´ə rāt´ing) *adj.* Thrilling; stimulating. page 102

ex•po•sure (ek spō´shər) *n.* The state of being visible or known. page 95

ex•pres•sive (ek spres´iv) *adj.* Able to show many emotions or meanings. Her expressive acting made people laugh, then weep. page 95

ex•ten•sive (ek sten´siv) *adj.* Great in range, distance, or amount. page 114

F

fau•na (fô´nə) *n.* Animal life. page 66

fear•less•ness (fîr´lis nis) *n.* Lack of fear. page 119

fig•ur•a•tive (fig´yər ə tiv) *adj.* Not literal. page 78

flo•ra (flôr´ə) *n.* Plant life. The desert flora is different from jungle plant life . page 66

fore•ground (fôr´ground´) *n.* The area in a picture closest to a viewer. page 13

for•mi•da•ble (fôr´mi də dəl) *adj.* Fearsome; difficult to overcome. page 109

for•ti•tude (fôr´ti tüd´, fôr´ti tūd´) *n.* Strength in difficult and dangerous situations. page 114

frag•ment•ed (frag´men tid) *adj.* Broken into pieces. page 61

fre•quen•cy (frē´kwən sē) *n.* **fre•quen•cies** The number of times; how often. page 42

fric•tion (frik´shən) *n.* The heat and strain caused when surfaces rub together. page 54

G

graph•ic (graf´ik) *adj.* Vivid; detailed. The graphic pictures of the distant planet amazed the scientists. page 30

H

half•heart•ed•ly (haf´här´tid lē) *adv.* In an unenthusiastic manner. page 60

hem•i•sphere (hem´i sfîr´) *n.* One half of the globe. page 54

he•ro•ic (hi rō´ik) *adj.* Having great courage. page 49

her•o•ism (her´ō is´əm) *n.* Conduct showing great courage and bravery. page 47

hu•man•kind (hū´mən kīnd´) *n.* All the people living on the earth. page 90

I

i•den•ti•cal (ī den´it kəl) *adj.* Exactly alike. Identical twins are hard to tell apart. page 78

i•den•ti•ty (ī den´ti tē) *n.* **i•den•ti•ties** All the things that make a specific person different from others. page 102

ig•ni•tion (ig nish´ən) *n.* Setting fire to something; the starting of an engine. page 12

im•meas•ur•a•ble (i mezh´ər ə bəl) *adj.* Too great to be measured. page 84

im•men•si•ty (i men´si tē) *n.* **im•men•si•ties** Great size. page 18

im•mor•tal•i•ty (im´ôr tal´i tē) *n.* Being remembered after death; life that never ends. page 47

im•pass•a•ble (im pas´ə bəl) *adj.* Impossible to travel through. The flooded road was impassable. page 109

im•pose (im pōz´) *v.* **im•posed, im•pos•ing** To force upon. It is silly to try to impose one's taste in music on others. page 78

im•pos•si•bil•i•ty (im pos´ə bil´i tē) *n.* **im•pos•si•bil•i•ties** Something that cannot happen or be. page 90

im•prac•ti•cal (im prak´ti kəl) *adj.* Not useful or efficient. page 78

im•prob•a•bil•i•ty (im prob´ə bil´i tē, im´prob ə bil´i tē) *n.* The state of being unlikely. page 68

im•prob•a•ble (im prob´ə bəl) *adj.* Unlikely. page 66

in•ad•e•quate (in ad´i kwit) *adj.* Not enough. page 71

in•di•ca•tion (in´di kā´shən) *n.* A sign. page 114

indus•tri•al•iz•ing (in dus´trē ə līz´ing) *adj.* Changing to an economy that relies on industry. page 36

in•ev•i•ta•ble (in ev´i tə bəl) *adj.* Certain to happen; not able to be avoided. page 18

in•fi•nite (in´fə nit) *adj.* Having no limits; endless. page 18

in•for•mal (in fôr´məl) *adj.* Not following any particular rules. page 30

in•hale (in hāl´) *v.* **in•haled, in•hal•ing** To breathe in. We inhaled the cold night air. page 119

in•quir•y (in kwir´ē, in´kwə rē) *n.* **inquiries** Investigation; research. page 18

in•stal•la•tion (in´stə lā´shən) *n.* The way something is set up and prepared for use. page 12

in•still (in stil´) *v.* To teach little by little. The teacher instilled a love of music in her students. page 95

in•stinc•tive•ly (in stingk´tiv lē) *adv.* Without thinking; on instinct. page 109

in•val•u•a•ble (in val´ū ə bəl, in val´yə bəl) *adj.* Important beyond price. page 18

in•volve•ment (in volv´ment) *n.* The act of taking part. page 95

K

knowl•edge•a•ble (nol´i jə bəl) *adj.* Knowing a great deal. page 6

L

leg•a•cy (leg´ə sē) *n.* **leg•a•cies** Heritage; what is received from earlier times. page 30

le•thal (lē´thəl) *adj.* Deadly. page 71

life•long (līf´lông´) *adj.* Lasting all through life. page 6

lit•er•al (lit´ər əl) *adj.* Basic; factual and exact. page 78

liv•a•ble (liv´ə bəl) *adj.* Able to support life. page 66

live (liv) *v.* **lived, liv•ing** To be alive. page 68

lore (lôr) *n.* Traditional knowledge. page 6

M

ma•neu•ver (mə nü´vər) *n.* A skillful move. page 114

mar•a•thon (mar´ə thon´) *n.* An extremely long race or contest. page 23

mel•an•chol•y (mel´ən kol´ē) *n.* **mel•an•chol•ies** Deep sadness; despair. The artist's melancholy showed in her paintings of sad people. page 30

merge (mûrg) *v.* **merged, merg•ing** To blend together. The two roads merged at the traffic light. page 109

mile•stone (mīl´stōn´) *n.* Something that marks a significant event. The first, tottering step is a milestone for a baby. page 47

min•gle (ming´gəl) *v.* **min•gled, min•gling** To mix together. page 60

moored (mùrd) *adj.* Fastened in place with ropes or anchors. page 61

O

ob•lit•er•ate (ə blit´ə rāt´) *v.* **ob•lit•er•at•ed, ob•lit•er•at•ing** To erase; to hide. page 61

out•burst (out´bûrst´) *n.* A sudden, violent act. page 85

o•ver•seas (ō´vər sēz´) *adj.* Across an ocean. page 90

P

pas•sion•ate (pash´ə nit) *adj.* Showing or feeling strong emotion. page 84

pas•tor•al (pas´tər əl) *adj.* Having to do with life in the country; peaceful. page 36

pil•grim•age (pil´grə mij) *n.* A journey for a special purpose. page 12

plum•met (plum´it) *v.* To fall suddenly. page 66

prec•i•pice (pres´ə pis) *n.* A very steep cliff. page 109

probe (prōb) *v.* **probed, prob•ing** To explore or investigate. page 18

pro•found (prə found´) *adj.* Deep. page 37

pro•fu•sion (prə fū´zhən) *n.* A great amount; abundance. The garden has a profusion of colorful flowers. page 36

pro•longed (prə lôngd´) *adj.* Extended. page 13

R

re•pent•ance (ri pent´təns) *n.* Deep regret for something one has done. page 85

ret•ro•spect (ret´rə spekt´) *n.* The act of looking back at the past. page 37

rev•er•ence (rev´ər əns, rev´rəns) *n.* Deep respect. page 42

rit•u•al (rich´ü əl) *n.* A set of actions repeated again and again. page 36

rup•ture (rup´chərd) *v.* **rup•tured, rup•tur•ing** To break open; to burst. page 60

S

seis•mic (sīz´mik) *adj.* Having to do with earthquakes. page 71

sen•si•tiv•i•ty (sen´si tiv´i tē) *n.* **sen•si•tiv•i•ties** Awareness, especially of others' feelings. page 37

sen•ti•ment (sen´tə mənt) *n.* Feeling. Giving someone a compliment shows the sentiment of caring. page 85

se•ver•i•ty (sə ver´i tē) *n.* **se•ver•i•ties** Harshness; intensity. page 54

sig•ni•fy (sig´nə fī´) *v.* **sig•ni•fied, sig•ni•fy•ing** To stand for; represent. page 78

smol•der•ing (smōl´dər ing) *adj.* Burning with little or no flame. page 61

stam•i•na (stam´ə nə) *n.* Strength and endurance. page 23

sur•mount (sər mount´) *v.* To climb to the top of; overcome. page 109

T

tan•gi•ble (tan´jə bəl) *adj.* Able to be touched. A rock is a tangible object. page 84

time•less (tīm´lis) *adj.* Unending; not changing with time. page 36

ti•tan•ic (tī tan´ik) *adj.* Enormous; powerful. page 13

trans•mit (trans mit´) *v.* **trans•mit•ted, trans•mit•ting** To send out. page 90

trek (trek) *n.* A slow, difficult journey. page 13

trem•or (trem´ər) *n.* A shaking, rolling motion of the ground; a shock to the earth's surface. page 54

tur•moil (tûr´moil) *n.* State of being in confusion; commotion. page 36

tus•sle (tus´əl) *n.* A struggle; a small fight. page 85

U

un•com•pre•hend•ing (un kom´pri hen´ding) *adj.* Not understanding. page 85

ur•ban•ite (ur´bə nīt´) *n.* A person who lives in the city. page 37

V

vet•er•an (vet´ər ən) *n.* A person who has served in the armed forces. page 47

vul•ner•a•ble (vul´nər ə bəl) *adj.* Able to be harmed. page 13

W

winch (winch) *v.* To raise by using a machine for pulling. page 60

Z

ze•nith (zē´nith) *n.* The point in the sky directly overhead. page 109

Answer Key

UNIT 1
STRETCHING BEYOND

LESSON 1
Dancing Across Time

CONTEXT CLUES
1. knowledgeable
2. ceremonial
3. diligent
4. anthropology
5. enriched
6. lore
7. derived
8. authentic
9. contemporary
10. lifelong

DICTIONARY SKILLS
1. anthropology: the science that studies human cultures and ways of life.
2. authentic: real; in agreement with fact.
3. ceremonial: having to do with a special occasion.
4. contemporary: belonging to the present time; current.
5. derived: came from a source or origin.
6. diligent: done with great care and effort.
7. enriched: made richer; added to.
8. knowledgeable: knowing a great deal.
9. lifelong: lasting all through life.
10. lore: traditional knowledge.

ANTONYMS
1. knowledge
2. authentic
3. diligent
4. contemporary
5. ceremonial
6. lifelong

RIDDLE
1. ceremonial
2. authentic
3. lore
4. anthropology
5. enriched
6. contemporary
7. lifelong
8. diligent
9. derived
10. knowledgeable
Answer to puzzle: they have two left feet.

GET WISE TO TESTS
1. B 3. A 5. D 7. D 9. B
2. C 4. A 6. C 8. A 10. C

WRITING
Answers will vary based on students' personal experiences.

LESSON 2
Earth Shine

CONTEXT CLUES
1. installation
2. prolonged
3. vulnerable
4. ignition
5. titanic
6. trek
7. diminishing
8. ascent
9. foreground
10. pilgrimage

WORD ORIGINS
1. ascent
2. ignition
3. diminishing
4. titanic
5. trek
6. vulnerable
7. prolonged

CLOZE PARAGRAPH
1. ignition
2. installation
3. pilgrimage
4. diminishing
5. foreground

GET WISE TO TESTS
1. C 3. C 5. A 7. D 9. A
2. A 4. D 6. B 8. C 10. B

Review
1. A 2. A 3. C 4. B

WRITING
Answers will vary based on students' personal experiences.

LESSON 3
New Views of the Universe

USING CONTEXT
1. analyze
2. immensity
3. cosmos
4. probe
5. inevitable
6. infinite
7. controversial
8. inquiry
9. invaluable
10. ascertain

CHALLENGE YOURSELF
Possible responses: waking up, breathing; elephants, whales; family, friends; whether people will live on other planets, how people will travel

DICTIONARY SKILLS
1. immensity
2. cosmos
3. cosmos
4. immensity, inevitable, infinite

REWRITING SENTENCES
1. My brother's help on this project was invaluable.
2. Once we have all of the information, we will analyze it.
3. The team's decision to elect a captain was controversial.
4. We need to ascertain how many people are coming to dinner.

GET WISE TO TESTS
1. D 3. C 5. A 7. C 9. D
2. C 4. B 6. D 8. A 10. B

WRITING
Answers will vary based on students' personal experiences.

LESSON 4
Setting Her Own Course

USING CONTEXT
1. marathon
2. aptitude
3. excel
4. stamina
5. acclaim
6. adverse
7. acute
8. dishearten
9. agonizing
10. aggressive

CHALLENGE YOURSELF
Possible responses: running, football; poverty, hunger; a poor grade, not being chosen for the baseball team; sports, playing an instrument

WORD GROUPS
1. adverse
2. aptitude
3. excel
4. aggressive
5. stamina
6. acute
7. dishearten
8. acclaim
9. marathon

ANTONYMS
1. acute
2. dishearten
3. agonizing
4. aggressive
5. excel
6. acclaim
7. stamina
8. adverse

WORD ORIGINS
1. excel
2. acute
3. agonizing
4. aptitude
5. adverse
6. aggressive
7. acclaim

CONNOTATIONS
1. stamina
2. aggressive
3. marathon
4. dishearten
5. acclaim

GET WISE TO TESTS
1. B 3. C 5. D 7. D 9. A
2. D 4. C 6. A 8. A 10. C

Review
1. C 2. B 3. D 4. C

WRITING
Answers will vary based on students' personal experiences.

UNIT 2 ART TALKS

LESSON 5
Portrait in Black

CONTEXT CLUES
1. biographical
2. informal
3. graphic
4. convey
5. ardent
6. emphasize
7. conscience
8. enlighten
9. melancholy
10. legacy

DICTIONARY SKILLS
1. convey, graphic
2. legacy
3. ardent, informal

WORD DESCRIPTIONS
1. ardent
2. emphasize
3. biographical
4. melancholy
5. conscience

CROSSWORD PUZZLE
Across
2. ardent
4. emphasize
5. melancholy
7. biographical
9. conscience
10. graphic

Down
1. legacy
3. enlighten
6. convey
8. informal

GET WISE TO TESTS
1. B 3. B 5. C 7. D 9. A
2. D 4. B 6. A 8. B 10. C

WRITING
Answers will vary based on students' personal experiences.

LESSON 6
Portrait of an Artist
USING CONTEXT
1. industrializing
2. urbanites
3. timeless
4. turmoil
5. pastoral
6. profound
7. profusion
8. retrospect
9. ritual
10. sensitivity

CHALLENGE YOURSELF
Possible responses: farm, animals; riots, unemployment; trees, plants

WORD ORIGINS
1. retrospect
2. ritual
3. urbanites
4. industrializing

REWRITING SENTENCES
1. The changing of the seasons is a timeless event.
2. He had a profound respect for his parents.
3. Her sensitivity to sounds caused her to avoid loud restaurants.
4. The speaker was surprised at the profusion of questions.
5. The civil war threw their country into turmoil.
6. She enjoyed showing the urbanites her country home.
7. I long to live in a pastoral place.

GET WISE TO TESTS
1. B 3. A 5. D 7. B 9. B
2. C 4. D 6. A 8. D 10. A

Review
1. B 2. D 3. B 4. D

WRITING
Answers will vary based on students' personal experiences.

LESSON 7
Buried Treasure
CONTEXT CLUES
1. archaeologists
2. excavate
3. bonanza
4. cultural
5. characteristic
6. frequency
7. descriptive
8. engravings
9. reverence
10. continuity

CHALLENGE YOURSELF
Possible responses: patriotism, optimism

ANALOGIES
1. characteristic
2. bonanza
3. reverence
4. archaeologists
5. excavate
6. engravings
7. continuity

CLOZE PARAGRAPH
1. archaeologists
2. engravings
3. descriptive
4. cultural
5. frequency
6. continuity

GET WISE TO TESTS
1. C 3. B 5. D 7. A 9. D
2. C 4. B 6. B 8. D 10. A

Review
1. C 2. A 3. D 4. B

WRITING
Answers will vary based on students' personal experiences.

LESSON 8
A New Peace
USING CONTEXT
1. dignifies
2. completion
3. veterans
4. heroism
5. immortality
6. architecture
7. authorized
8. milestone
9. eligible
10. creativity

CHALLENGE YOURSELF
Possible responses: Declaration of Independence, moon landing; Martin Luther King, Jr., Johnny Tremain; dancer, architect; Empire State Building, White House

WORD GROUPS
1. heroism
2. authorized
3. veterans
4. dignifies
5. eligible
6. creativity
7. architecture
8. milestone

WORD PAIRS
Answers will vary based on students' personal experiences.

WORD MAP
What the Designer Had to Be or Have: creativity; authorized, eligible
What the Memorial Stands For: heroism, immortality
Who Visits the Memorial: veterans
How Visitors Seeing the Memorial Feel: additional answers will vary.

GET WISE TO TESTS
1. B 3. A 5. D 7. A 9. D
2. D 4. C 6. B 8. C 10. A

Review
1. C 2. B 3. A 4. B

WRITING
Answers will vary based on students' personal experiences.

UNIT 3
THE EARTH IS MOVING!

LESSON 9
Quake, Tremble, and Roll
CONTEXT CLUES
1. friction
2. audible
3. contour
4. tremor
5. severity
6. disrupts
7. crucial
8. destructive
9. hemisphere
10. exert

REWRITING SENTENCES
1. This hemisphere has active earthquake areas.
2. The contour of the shore can be changed by an earthquake.
3. We felt the first tremor.
4. The friction of the giant plates was building rapidly.
5. The plates exert pressure on one another.

CONNOTATIONS
1. destructive
2. severity
3. crucial
4. disrupts

TANGLED-UP WORDS
1. tremor
2. audible
3. severity
4. hemisphere
5. crucial
6. exert
7. destructive
8. contour
9. friction
10. disrupted

GET WISE TO TESTS
1. C 3. A 5. C 7. A 9. D
2. D 4. D 6. B 8. C 10. B

Review
1. D 2. C

WRITING
Answers will vary based on students' personal experiences.

LESSON 10
The Shark Callers
USING CONTEXT
1. moored
2. winch
3. obliterate
4. halfheartedly
5. mingled
6. ruptured
7. fragmented
8. dormant
9. coursed
10. smoldering

CHALLENGE YOURSELF
Possible responses: glass, chalk; logs, charcoal pieces; wake up, do chores; a machine, emotions

WORD GROUPS
1. fragmented
2. coursed
3. smoldering
4. ruptured
5. winch
6. dormant
7. mingled
8. moored
9. dormant
10. obliterate

ANTONYMS
1. halfheartedly
2. obliterate
3. dormant
4. fragmented
5. moored
6. mingled

GET WISE TO TESTS
1. C 3. A 5. B 7. D 9. D
2. B 4. D 6. C 8. A 10. B

Review
1. D 2. B 3. A 4. B 5. A

WRITING
Answers will vary based on students' personal experiences.

LESSON 11
A Mountain of Surprises
CONTEXT CLUES
1. adjoining
2. flora
3. fauna
4. plummeted
5. blighted
6. altered
7. improbable
8. livable
9. disastrous
10. cope

ANALOGIES
1. cope
2. improbable
3. fauna
4. plummeted
5. adjoining
6. blighted
7. flora

WORD PAIRS
Answers will vary based on students' personal experiences.

GET WISE TO TESTS
1. D 3. C 5. B 7. B 9. D
2. B 4. C 6. D 8. C 10. A

Review
1. B 2. A 3. C 4. D

WRITING
Answers will vary based on students' personal experiences.

LESSON 12
How Big? How Serious?
CONTEXT CLUES
1. inadequate 6. evaluate
2. lethal 7. accuracy
3. devastate 8. compute
4. contributor 9. anticipate
5. seismic 10. avert

WORD GROUPS
1. lethal 4. compute
2. devastate 5. contributor
3. anticipate 6. evaluate

DICTIONARY SKILLS
1. inadequate, b 4. accuracy, b
2. anticipate, a 5. avert, b
3. contributor, a

WORD GAME
1. inadequate 6. accuracy
2. anticipate 7. seismic
3. contributor 8. evaluate
4. devastate 9. compute
5. lethal 10. averted

GET WISE TO TESTS
1. B 3. B 5. B 7. C 9. A
2. D 4. C 6. A 8. C 10. D

Review
1. D 2. C

WRITING
Answers will vary based on students' personal experiences.

UNIT 4 SENDING MESSAGES

LESSON 13
Writing with Symbols
CONTEXT CLUES
1. figurative 6. impractical
2. bewildering 7. signify
3. characters 8. Excluding
4. literal 9. imposing
5. dialects 10. identical

CHALLENGE YOURSELF
Possible responses: Blue means feeling sad.

WORD ORIGINS
1. dialects 5. literal
2. identical 6. impractical
3. bewildering 7. figurative
4. signify 8. characters

MULTIPLE MEANINGS
1. 3 2. 4 3. 2 4. 1

TANGLED-UP WORDS
1. bewildering 6. impractical
2. dialects 7. identical
3. excluding 8. imposing
4. signify 9. literal
5. characters 10. figurative

GET WISE TO TESTS
1. A 3. C 5. A 7. B 9. D
2. C 4. C 6. C 8. A 10. D

Review
1. D 2. A

WRITING
Answers will vary based on students' personal experiences.

LESSON 14
The Story of My Life
CONTEXT CLUES
1. immeasurable 6. uncomprehending
2. eventful 7. outburst
3. bitterness 8. tangible
4. passionate 9. repentance
5. tussle 10. sentiment

ANALOGIES
1. passionate 4. eventful
2. tussle 5. tangible
3. bitterness

CLOZE PARAGRAPH
1. outburst 5. tangible
2. uncomprehending 6. tussle
3. sentiment 7. repentance
4. immeasurable

GET WISE TO TESTS
1. D 3. A 5. A 7. B 9. B
2. C 4. C 6. C 8. D 10. C

Review
1. B 2. B 3. D 4. A 5. C

WRITING
Answers will vary based on students' personal experiences.

LESSON 15
A Smaller World
USING CONTEXT
1. amazingly 6. overseas
2. contraptions 7. correspondence
3. humankind 8. transmit
4. clarity 9. exceeded
5. impossibility 10. closeness

CHALLENGE YOURSELF
Possible responses: Italy, Japan; can opener, popcorn maker; peace, enough food; travel in space, talk on telephone

ANTONYMS
1. closeness 4. Amazingly
2. Overseas 5. clarity
3. impossibility 6. transmit

WRITING SENTENCES
Answers will vary based on students' personal experiences.

GET WISE TO TESTS
1. C 3. A 5. B 7. D 9. A
2. A 4. D 6. C 8. D 10. C

Review
1. B 3. C 5. C
2. A 4. B 6. A

WRITING
Answers will vary based on students' personal experiences.

LESSON 16
Many Talents, Many Faces
USING CONTEXT
1. conventional 6. expressive
2. instill 7. acceptance
3. exposure 8. confined
4. disadvantage 9. ethnic
5. involvement 10. evoke

CHALLENGE YOURSELF
Possible responses: listening well, studying hard; by bus, by bicycle; playing on local sports teams, attending town events; hitting a home run, striking out a batter

ANTONYMS
1. expressive 5. conventional
2. disadvantage 6. evoke
3. confined 7. instill
4. acceptance

CLOZE PARAGRAPH
exposure   disadvantage
ethnic   conventional
instill   involvement

WORD ORIGINS
1. acceptance 4. confined
2. exposure 5. instill
3. evoke 6. ethnic

WRITING SENTENCES
Answers will vary based on students' personal experiences.

GET WISE TO TESTS
1. B 3. D 5. C 7. B 9. A
2. C 4. A 6. C 8. A 10. C

WRITING
Answers will vary based on students' personal experiences.

UNIT 5
SPIRIT OF ADVENTURE

LESSON 17
Wonder Woman
CONTEXT CLUES
1. disability 6. assurance
2. acrobatics 7. adversity
3. identify 8. ace
4. coordination 9. antics
5. agility 10. exhilarating

CONNOTATIONS
1. ace 4. acrobatics
2. adversity 5. exhilarating
3. antics 6. identify

WORD PAIRS
Answers will vary based on students' personal experiences.

WORD MAP
What Stunt Performers Do: acrobatics, antics Qualities of Stunt Performers: agility, coordination
Terms that Describe Stunt Performers: ace How Audiences Might Describe Stunt Performers: exhilarating

GET WISE TO TESTS
1. C 3. A 5. B 7. C 9. B
2. A 4. D 6. C 8. A 10. C

Review
1. B   2. D

WRITING
Answers will vary based on students' personal experiences.

LESSON 18
Banner in the Sky

CONTEXT CLUES
1. formidable   6. impassable
2. committed   7. merged
3. surmount   8. instinctively
4. precipice   9. bracing
5. abyss   10. zenith

CHALLENGE YOURSELF
Possible responses: complete assignment, make new friends; sneeze, yawn

ANALOGIES
1. committed   4. precipice
2. formidable   5. surmount
3. abyss   6. merged

WORD DESCRIPTIONS
1. bracing   4. zenith
2. impassable   5. instinctively
3. surmount

GET WISE TO TESTS
1. D   3. C   5. A   7. C   9. A
2. A   4. A   6. D   8. D   10. C

Review
1. D   2. C   3. B   4. D

WRITING
Answers will vary based on students' personal experiences.

LESSON 19
West Through the Night

CONTEXT CLUES
1. emotional   6. commitment
2. extensive   7. indication
3. diligence   8. maneuver
4. conceded   9. esteem
5. competent   10. fortitude

WORD ORIGINS
1. diligence   4. maneuver
2. esteem   5. commitment
3. conceded   6. emotional

REWRITING SENTENCES
1. That maneuver may win him the chess championship.
2. She has the fortitude to reach her goal.
3. The mayor presented extensive plans to help the homeless.
4. We hold our teacher in esteem.
5. A child is not competent to drive a school bus.
6. There is no indication that the blizzard will hit this area.

GET WISE TO TESTS
1. B   3. D   5. B   7. C   9. A
2. D   4. D   6. A   8. D   10. A

Review
1. B   2. D   3. A   4. C   5. B

WRITING
Answers will vary based on students' personal experiences.

LESSON 20
Underwater Explorer

USING CONTEXT
1. colleagues   6. cooperation
2. array   7. exhale
3. inhale   8. dominant
4. fearlessness   9. environmental
5. adviser   10. confronted

CHALLENGE YOURSELF
Possible responses: newspaper, drama club; class play, orchestra; air pollution, water pollution

CLOZE PARAGRAPH
1. colleagues   6. confronted
2. adviser   7. fearlessness
3. inhale   8. array
4. exhale   9. environmental
5. cooperation   10. dominant

WORD GAME
1. environmental   6. adviser
2. inhale   7. dominant
3. cooperation   8. confronted
4. fearlessness   9. colleagues
5. array   10. exhale

GET WISE TO TESTS
1. A   3. B   5. D   7. D   9. B
2. C   4. D   6. A   8. A   10. D

Review
1. A   2. C   3. D   4. D

WRITING
Answers will vary based on students' personal experiences.

UNIT 1 REVIEW
1. ascertain   7. knowledgeable
2. vulnerable   8. cosmos
3. anthropology   9. ignition
4. excel   10. diminishing
5. adverse   11. controversial
6. enriched   12. stamina

UNIT 2 REVIEW
1. yes   9. yes
2. no   10. no
3. yes   11. no
4. no   12. no
5. yes   13. yes
6. yes   14. no
7. no   15. yes
8. yes

UNIT 3 REVIEW
1. halfheartedly   7. inadequate
2. fauna   8. altered
3. disrupts   9. disastrous
4. anticipate   10. seismic
5. hemisphere   11. winch
6. audible   12. mingled

UNIT 4 REVIEW
1. no   9. no
2. no   10. yes
3. no   11. no
4. yes   12. yes
5. no   13. yes
6. yes   14. no
7. no   15. no
8. no

UNIT 5 REVIEW
1. coordination   7. emotional
2. exhilarating   8. exhale
3. zenith   9. commitment
4. esteem   10. instinctively
5. confronted   11. antics
6. merged   12. array

REVIEW AND WRITE
Answers will vary based on students' personal experiences.